How Many Things
Can You
Do
in the Nude?

How Many Things Can You Do in the Nude?

by Ray Reese

EVEREST
HOUSE
Publishers

New York

Library of Congress Cataloging in Publication Data:

Reese, Ray.   How many things can you do in the nude?
1. Questions and answers. I. Title.
AG195.R43   1981   031'.02   81-12662
ISBN: 0-89696-116-8 (pbk.)   AACR2

Published simultaneously in Canada by
Beaverbooks, Don Mills, Ontario
Manufactured in the United States of America
Designed by Suzanne Haldane

To my mother and father, Dorothy and Harry Reese.
To Sue, and most of all for my son, Douglas, the
very best thing that ever happened to me.

Contents

Acknowledgments

One of the first things everyone asks when you complete a project such as this is, "How the hell did you get to all those people?" There are many ways. You can siphon the gas out of Cher's car and then just kind of pull up casually and ask if there is anything you can do to help. Tripping and falling prostrate across Burt Reynolds's table at Sardi's is also good, provided that you are accomplished enough to destroy the table without actually getting any food on Mr. Reynolds's expensive suit.

A willingness to throw oneself in front of passing limousines with tinted windows, on the chance that someone worth meeting may be inside, is admirable, but having a friend who works for the phone company is even better.

Other than that, one must depend on old friends and, as Blanche DuBois so often said, the kindness of strangers.

What follows, then, is an incomplete list of those without whom this book might have been possible, but certainly not probable.

First, a special thank-you to my editor, Bill Thompson, who has a way of leaving you alone until you discover that he was right all along; and of course, as always, to my agents, Steve Dansky and Bret Adams.

Grateful appreciation is extended to Kimberly Staunch, David Petitto, John Moranville, Jan McCormack, Joel Stein, John Dorsey, Joe and Helen Seiter, Lillie and Harry Greer, John Greer, Jerry Modine, George Smith,

Liza Minnelli, Norma Reese, Ruby, Henry, and Lee
Miller, Glenard and Eva Reece, Opal and Joseph Rubel,
Sallie and Louis Halter, and Lowell and Elizabeth Brown,
all of whom know how much they contributed. For their
gallant efforts on my behalf, my thanks to Mike
Cantalupo, Catherine Donoghue Hartman, Regine, Burt
Reynolds, Caren Tauber, Judith Lerner, Flo Selfman,
Doug Taylor, Myrna Huffman, and the wizards at
Celebrity Service in Hollywood, New York, London, and
Paris. Finally, credit where more than credit is due to the
telephone company's "411" operators, the Canadian Office
of Tourism, and to the assembled students of the
University of Michigan at Ann Arbor, the University of
Texas at Austin, the University of Missouri at Columbia,
the University of Washington at St. Louis, the University
of California at Los Angeles, the University of Southern
California, Harvard, Yale, Sarah Lawrence, Bryn Mawr,
the U.S. Naval Academy, the Parsons School of Design,
and Le Cordon Bleu de Paris.

A SPECIAL ACKNOWLEDGMENT

Michael Kohan is among that rarest of breeds in this
disposable age who still gets excited by whatever it is
he happens to be doing. He has functioned here as
researcher, photographer, travel coordinator and the
person in charge of everything else that needed to be
done.

During the course of these interviews, he dined
with Peter Ustinov, laughed with George Carlin and
letched with Candice Bergen.

All in all, I think he was overpaid!

Foreword

Hotel de Paris,
Monaco

To be almost honest, this book began late one night, on an Air France jet, somewhere between Paris and New York, as a ruse to meet Margaux Hemingway, who was seated just across the aisle.

Since then, I have traveled halfway around the world and back, and back again, interviewing some two hundred of the brightest, most talented people in that world. People who, for one reason or another, are considered among the very best at what they do.

Some were old friends, to whom I owe a debt of gratitude. Many more are cherished new acquaintances. Almost all were exceedingly gracious. A few were a pain in the ass.

Long ago, Doctor Watson used to invent games to amuse himself and sharpen the ever-ready wit of his companion Mister Holmes, during those long train trips through the misting Scottish moors.

This book is intended for precisely the same purpose. These are not games which someone must win. If you should happen to emerge victorious here in a thrilling duel with George Carlin or Helen Gurley Brown no one will ever believe you anyway.

Each chapter is built around a question which was posed to one or more of our celebrities. In most cases you will find the celebrities' answer immediately following. Score yourself according to the instructions accompanying each test. You will soon discover that if you write your answers lightly and erase carefully you can easily recoup the price of the book by winning incredible bar bets (and earning the undying hatred of almost everyone you meet).

These interviews were conducted mostly in person, during a hectic period of some five months. With the possible exception of an extended drinking spree in London that resulted in it taking me three days to find where I had parked the car, the experience has been an enjoyable one.

So after hundreds of hours of research and interviews, missed planes and crossed wires and the charming child in the marble palazzo in Venice who kept kicking me when his famous mother wasn't looking, I invite you to challenge Rex Reed, match wits with Peter Ustinov, do battle with Art Buchwald at his best. Come on, test yourself against the experts!

HOW MANY THINGS CAN YOU DO IN THE NUDE?

How Many Things Can You Do In The Nude?

1:46 A.M.
McCarran Field
Las Vegas, Nevada

This is Las Vegas. It is 1:46 A.M. Not five hours ago I was completely sane. I had just concluded interviewing the last of a long and impressive list of Las Vegas's top headliners, talked myself out of just one more valiant try at getting past Goldie Hawn's manager, finished my third martini, and decided to take the rest of the night off and just relax. Nothing to do until I caught the plane tomorrow for New York.

Then it happened.

I was walking through the casino, barely three minutes late for our dinner reservation, not ten feet from where Michael Kohan, my assistant, stood waiting with the smiling maitre d' inside the beckoning door of DaVinci's, when the overhead loudspeaker crackled:

". . . Ray Reese . . . Long distance telephone for Ray Reese . . ."

Nodding to Michael to go ahead, I took the call on the house phone. It was from New York, informing me that we might be able to get Alexis Smith, star of the touring company of Broadway's *The Best Little Whorehouse in Texas,* if we could make connections with her on the road.

What an interview that would make! I was ecstatic! I had been madly in love with Alexis Smith

17

for years. It was the perfect ending to an imperfect day. Now I could enjoy my dinner!

Smiling, I got even closer to the distinguished-looking maitre d' waiting in the doorway when suddenly my eye was drawn to the headline on the inside page of the *Las Vegas Review-Journal* that some guy was reading at the bar: THE BEST LITTLE WHOREHOUSE IN TEXAS IS IN NEVADA!

Offering the stranger two silver dollars for his paper, I scanned the article quickly. It seems that The Chicken Ranch Brothel, which was the inspiration for the Broadway show, had been forced to leave Texas and was now operating legally right here, in Nevada.

Fingers crossed, and without thinking about how it would sound, I dialed the Maxim Hotel switchboard, told them that this was an emergency, and asked if they could put me through to the Chicken Ranch Brothel in Parumph, Nevada!

The telephone danced with static in my ear. The connection was made and I attempted to explain to the voice on the other end that I was doing this enormously important celebrity book, and that we had interviewed everyone from the Dalai Lama to Xaviera Hollander, and were now on our way to interview Alexis Smith, I thought that it might be a good idea if we could come out and interview the "originals," so to speak.

Silence. Then static. She isn't impressed. Behind me, the guy from the bar has just turned my two bucks into $300 at the slot machine.

"Damn!" Whatever made me think they would buy someone calling up in the middle of the night babbling about some book and . . .

"Mr. Reese?"

"Yes!"

"It's going to be awfully late by the time you drive all the way out here, so . . . why don't we send a plane for you?"

18

Clicking the receiver frantically, I begged for the Maxim operator.

"Can you page Michael Kohan in the DaVinci restaurant? Tell him to stop whatever it is he's doing, get upstairs and unpack, grab his camera and tape recorder, and meet me in the airport in five minutes?"

This is Las Vegas. It is now 2 A.M. I am standing on the runway in 35 M.P.H. gusting winds. The plane bouncing toward me is a single-engine Cessna.

I can see the headline in *The New York Times*: SEMI-FAMOUS AUTHOR DIES ON WAY TO WHOREHOUSE IN PARUMPH, NEVADA!

Ultimately, I missed Alexis Smith in New York and in London, catching up with her finally, but only when the maitre d' at Martoni's in Hollywood seated her at the table next to mine.

ALEXIS SMITH	*"Oh! Calcutta!"*
DAVID BRENNER	Apologize!
PETER USTINOV	Get born!
MARILYN CHAMBERS	Me!
RANCHHAND JENNIFER	Work!
MILTON BERLE	Sell Insurance
ELIZABETH ASHLEY	Contemplate your navel!
LUCIE ARNAZ	Play doctor
BEN VEREEN	Flash!
RANCHHAND TERRI	Your nails
BRETT SOMERS	Screw!
ART BUCHWALD	Become a nudist!
BILL CULLEN	X-rated movies
GENE RAYBURN	Get cremated!
TONY DANZA	Skinny dip!
JOEL GREY	Shower
MARILU HENNER	*Playboy* centerfolds

RANCHHAND	
MONIQUE	Play strip poker
MIKE DOUGLAS	Take a physical
TONY ORLANDO	Play doctor
JUDITH KRANTZ	Sleep
GEORGE BURNS	Call room service
PAT HARRINGTON	Make love
REGINE	Make babies
ED ASNER	Explore
RICHARD HATCH	Streak!
PETER MARSHALL	Radio show
DR. JOYCE BROTHERS	Get excited!
BETTY WHITE	Start a diet!
GALLAGHER	Nothing!
CRYSTAL GAYLE	Giggle
FRANCESCO SCAVULLO	Get arrested
MADELINE KAHN	Perform an unnatural act
CHARLENE TILTON	Sing in the shower
REX REED	Get dressed

20

Things People Normally Put Their Fingers Into

✳

I asked almost all of our celebrities this question, and, as you might imagine, many of the responses were unusual—or unprintable. The key word here is *normally;* we are looking for answers like "fingerpaints" or "their pockets." Score 1 point for each correct answer and 2 points for anything the celebrities overlooked.

Here is my choice of 50 of the best answers we received, including two or three that earned no points but were just too good to pass up.

JOEL GREY	Telephone dials
CALVIN KLEIN	Scissors
PETER USTINOV	Holy water
BETTY WHITE	Yo-yo strings
DR. JOYCE BROTHERS	The Yellow Pages
BEN VEREEN	Thimbles
JED ALLEN	Key chains
ELIZABETH ASHLEY	Your lover's hair
GENE RAYBURN	Dikes
DR. IRENE KASSORLA	Popcorn
MADELINE KAHN	Fingerpaints

DAVID BRENNER	Bowling balls
LUCIE ARNAZ	Gloves
RICHARD HATCH	Poi
FRED GRANDY	The Lennon Sisters
JAMES KOMACK	Other people
MARK GOODSON	Fingerbowls
REX REED	Splints
BILL CULLEN	Their ears
BOB HOPE	Wet paint
THE DUKE OF BEDFORD	Envelopes
TWIGGY	Shampoo
JIMMY BRESLIN	Exhaust pipes
JOYCE BULIFANT	Your friends
DICK MARTIN	Belt loops
DICK VAN PATTEN	Dishwater
MARY BETH McDONOUGH	Purses
JOANNA CASSIDY	Their mouths
DEAN JONES	Their coatsleeves
PETER MARSHALL	Car door handles
SHARI LEWIS	Finger puppets
KURT RUSSELL	Golf greens
BOBBY VINTON	Light sockets
PATRICK TERRAIL	Harp strings
GALLAGHER	Mud pies
TONY ORLANDO	Their pockets
PAT HARRINGTON	Manicurist's bowl
LAURIE WALTERS	Clay
GEORGE HAMILTON	A trigger guard
FRANCESCO SCAVULLO	Coffee-cup handles
SHIELDS AND YARNELL	The cookie jar
MAUREEN McCORMICK	Luggage handles
CHARLES NELSON REILLY	Pipe bowls

JOYCE SELZNICK	Chinese handcuffs
BILL DAILY	Their noses
WYOMIA TYUS	Bathwater
STEVE ALLEN	Cake icing
BRUCE FORSYTH	Cat's cradle
SIR FREDDIE LAKER	The wind
MORT SAHL	An abacus
GEORGE BURNS	Brass knuckles
SAMMY DAVIS, JR.	Rings
MARILYN CHAMBERS	Me!

Twenty Things You Wouldn't Want to Be Caught Doing

Mort Sahl

If you were a World War II fighter pilot in a flaming B-52 bomber about to crash on the coast of France, Mort Sahl is the kind of guy who would sit in the copilot's seat and talk a little faster so that he could make his point before you hit the ground.

Stranger yet, you'd probably find yourself interested in what he had to say.

In the last 30 seconds he has quoted Stan Kenton, Justice William O. Douglas, Adlai Stevenson, and Miz Lillian. The subjects fly past like telephone poles in a Burt Reynolds movie.

I ask him who or what makes Mort Sahl laugh.

MORT   Bob Hope is the greatest living satirist in America today. Nobody can touch him! A lot of people on the left, who disagree with his politics won't like that, but politics and talent are two separate things.

RAY   "You once said that as your New Year's resolution you were going to give up dating actresses and other female impersonators.

MORT   That's a good line . . . I just don't think that "tough" and "feminine" are mutually exclusive. You gotta listen when Germaine Greer talks. If you don't she'll punch your lights out!

RAY   Whom do you like? Who are your heroes?

MORT   It's tough. Stan Kenton, he was like a father. John Hendricks, because he makes me smile. Justice Douglas and Adlai Stevenson. John Fitzgerald Kennedy.

RAY   You still didn't tell me; Who makes Mort Sahl laugh?

MORT   Not John Belushi. Not Gilda Radner. Not Steve Martin.

I asked Mort to name some THINGS YOU WOULDN'T BE CAUGHT DOING. I've selected just 20 of his and our other celebrities' best responses, but before you peek, try your own hand at it. Relax! There is absolutely no way to prepare. This category was suggested to me by something that Mort said as we were sitting in his office one day discussing the psychological impact of Suzanne Somers on future generations.

Take 1 point for each answer you think of. There's a 1-point bonus if you come up with something they did.

MORT SAHL	Watching "Sheriff Lobo"
PETER USTINOV	Thy neighbor's wife
ED ASNER	Cheating on your income tax
BRETT SOMERS	Reading the *National Enquirer*
BILL CULLEN	Breaking all of the commandments, twice

Joyce Bulifant

JIMMY KOMACK	In bed with Jim Brown's old lady
TONY DANZA	With your finger in your nose
PATRICK TERRAIL	With your hand in the till
GENE RAYBURN	Shoplighting something cheap
MARILYN CHAMBERS	Faking it
DAVID BRENNER	Making obscene calls to Phyllis Diller
FRED GRANDY	Wearing rubber
DR. JOYCE BROTHERS	Littering
BETTY WHITE	Cheating
JED ALLEN	Committing adultery
RUTH GORDON	Lying
BOBBY SHORT	Telling secrets
JOYCE BULIFANT	Squeezing the Charmin
ELIZABETH ASHLEY	Voting for Ronald Reagan
ELAINE JOYCE	John Belushi
PETER MARSHALL	Masturbating

Things You Blow

Now I know that some of you probably think I'm having fun, flying all over the place, talking and drinking with some of the world's brightest people. Oh sure, it looks good at first glance. But it's not all fun and games. I have to get a book out. Consider:

I am lying on a private beach in southern Florida. Marilyn Chambers is sunbathing, topless, on the same beach.

She has just asked me if I would mind applying oil to the places she can't reach. Ms. Chambers arches her back as I reach out to touch her, oil in hand.

In this instant I ask Marilyn Chambers if she could think of some THINGS YOU BLOW.

No clues this time. You'll just have to depend on your own overactive imagination. I should point out that the ground rules only allow you to name one musical instrument.

Ms. Chambers came up with 28 acceptable answers.

Give yourself 3 points for each answer you come up with.

Barely pausing to take a deep breath, Marilyn gave us the following:

You know what
Balloons
Your own horn
Your top
Musical instruments
You blow up paper bags
You blow out birthday
   candles
Your nose
Your big chance
In your lover's ear
Pinwheels
New Year's Eve
   noisemakers

Into a breathometer
Blow on fingernail polish
Money in Las Vegas
You blow on dandelions
You blow-dry your hair
On hot coffee
Bubbles
Bubble gum
You blow up tires
Your mind
Away eraser dust
You blow out matches
Things out of proportion
Rape whistles

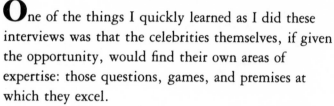

Things That Hold
Things Up

The Plaza Hotel
New York

One of the things I quickly learned as I did these interviews was that the celebrities themselves, if given the opportunity, would find their own areas of expertise: those questions, games, and premises at which they excel.

No one as easily found that niche as did Betty White, David Brenner, and Elizabeth Ashley. All three were incredible when given a premise to which they could react off the top of their heads, with no time to discard one answer in favor of a better one. Though I spoke to the three people separately, I have taken some of their best answers and interwoven them, as an example of how three very different minds approach the same subject.

After you have had the opportunity to match wits with Betty, David, and Elizabeth and then checked your answers against theirs, check out the responses provided by members of the senior creative writing class at UCLA.

This might be a good time to point out that all of the celebrities interviewed for this book were faced with the pressures of limited time, flashing cameras, whirring tape recorders, occasional agents, press agents, and me, all waiting for them to say something brilliant. The simple luxury of not having anyone there staring at you as you try to concentrate should

Betty White

David Brenner

Elizabeth Ashley

give you a big head start, so here is your question. See if you can think of some THINGS THAT HOLD THINGS UP, like *belts . . . rafters . . . detours*.

DAVID	Denture cream
BETTY	The IRS
ELIZABETH	Platform shoes
DAVID	Airplanes
BETTY	Red tape
ELIZABETH	Parachutes
DAVID	Necks
BETTY	The hangman's noose
ELIZABETH	Safety pins
DAVID	Thumbtacks
BETTY	Car jacks
ELIZABETH	Jock straps
DAVID	Crutches
BETTY	Cables and cable cars
ELIZABETH	Bookshelves
DAVID	Tires and flat tires
BETTY	Bulletin boards
ELIZABETH	Airport security checks
DAVID	Filibusters
BETTY	Curtain rods
ELIZABETH	Boats
DAVID	Yo-yo strings
BETTY	King Kong
ELIZABETH	Foreplay
DAVID	Girders and girdles
BETTY	Chastity belts
ELIZABETH	Coat hangers
DAVID	Bridges
BETTY	Brassieres
ELIZABETH	Picture hooks
DAVID	Ladders
BETTY	A truss
ELIZABETH	Scaffolds

DAVID	Noses hold up eyeglasses
BETTY	Traffic jams
ELIZABETH	Telephone poles
DAVID	Suspenders
BETTY	Garters
ELIZABETH	Garter belts
DAVID	Virgins
BETTY	Bar stools
ELIZABETH	Helium
DAVID	Balancing acts
BETTY	Bed frames
ELIZABETH	Bonnie and Clyde

Here is a list of additional answers provided to us by the members of the senior creative writing class at UCLA.

Nails and tacks	Foundations
Tape	Canes
Pushpins	Macramé hangers
Elevators	Footstools
Hot-air balloons	Hassocks
Gliders	Stirrups
Hooks	Traffic jams
Running boards	Bolts
Running out of gas	Screws
Platforms	Dowels
Stairs	Arms
Guns	Hands
Straps	Pretty Boy Floyd
Tables	Steps
Credenza	Detours
Beams	Saddles
Braces (both kinds)	Bored waiters
Walls	Strikes
Chains	Jesse James

Things That Put You Down

Ed Asner

Mort Sahl

Now that you're getting the general idea, let's try it again. The secret is to let your mind roam through all the possible interpretations of the question. See if you can think of THINGS THAT PUT YOU DOWN.

This time I have chosen just twenty of the best answers from our own celebrities.

Score 5 points for each answer you match with our celebrities. Take 2 points for anything that they overlooked.

JED ALLEN	Critics
MARILU HENNER	Elevators
REX REED	Don Rickles
DICK VAN PATTEN	Escalators
ED ASNER	Teeter-totters
MARILYN CHAMBERS	The flu
MIKE DOUGLAS	Dear John letters
DAVID NIVEN	Parachutes
MORT SAHL	Martin Scorsese movies
ELIZABETH ASHLEY	The blues
CALVIN KLEIN	Playground slides
MILTON BERLE	Barber chairs
DICK MARTIN	Dexedrine

Peter Ustinov

Elizabeth Ashley

JIM LANGE	Insults
BIANCA JAGGER	Airplanes
JOEL GREY	Fire escapes
ART BUCHWALD	Submarines
JIMMY BRESLIN	Muhammad Ali
PETER USTINOV	Ski jumps
DR. JOYCE BROTHERS	Undertakers

Things You Kiss

I find myself in a dressing room at CBS, a tiny room perhaps 10 by 12 feet unsquare. There are 17 of us crowded into this room: 15 and a half if you consider that Michael is half out in the hall with his cameras and tape recorders and Betty White is perched on the arm of the sofa, not actually taking up any floor space.

Let me introduce those present. On the love seat we have Dick Martin, Brett Somers, and Charles Nelson Reilly. Seated on the end table, next to Brett, is Ira Skutch, producer of "The Match Game," and on the large sofa are Gene Rayburn, Elaine Joyce, Bill Cullen, Louise Sorel, and of course Betty White, hovering on the armrest. The floor is carpeted with Peter Marshall, Joyce Bulifant, Richard Deacon, Bill Daily, myself, and Fred Grandy, who plays Gopher on "Love Boat." Fred's wife, Jan, is hidden back there somewhere, or was the last time I looked.

Taking a deep breath I decide to dispense with any in-depth explanation of what this interview is for; I am just about to ask the first question when Brett Somers beats me to it. "This interview is for a book?" she asks, nodding toward the tape recorder.

"Yes . . ."

"Well, my favorite color is blue, my favorite food is caviar, and if you want to know what I sleep

34

in, I sleep in the arms of whoever the hell happens to be there at the moment!"

"What I really want to know is whether you can think of some things you kiss."

"Sure. . . . Are you ready?"

"Yes."

"Kiss off!!"

As you can see, you're in dangerous territory now. There was enough talent in that little room, everyone shouting out answers at the same time, to make my faithful Japanese tape recorder consider hara-kiri. Call a friend, or ask the postman to help you—you're going to need it.

You get 3 points for each answer.

*Brett Somers
& Dick Martin*

Louise Sorel

BETTY WHITE	Babies
LOUISE SOREL	Babies' bottoms
PETER MARSHALL	Bo Derek's bottom
GENE RAYBURN	Bo Derek's top
ELAINE JOYCE	Grandma and Grandpa
CHARLES NELSON REILLY	. . . me Kate
RICHARD DEACON	Mommy and Daddy
JOYCE BULIFANT	Kissin' cousins
BRETT SOMERS	Customers in a kissing booth
BILL CULLEN	. . . and make up
BETTY WHITE	Strangers on New Year's Eve
DICK MARTIN	Motorcycle policemen
BILL DAILY	The ground after a bad flight
BRETT SOMERS	Robert Redford
BILL DAILY	What she said!
FRED GRANDY	Mafia hit men

Peter Marshall

PETER MARSHALL	The bride
DICK MARTIN	The bridesmaids
BILL DAILY	People kiss dogs!
BILL CULLEN	Lips
LOUISE SOREL	Ears
BETTY WHITE	Cheeks
GENE RAYBURN	You kiss the hostess
FRED GRANDY	. . . your dreams goodbye
JOYCE BULIFANT	Your husband
BETTY WHITE	Other people's husbands
PETER MARSHALL	Your wife
DICK MARTIN	Your mistress
BILL CULLEN	Old friends
BRETT SOMERS	. . . on the first date
RICHARD DEACON	. . . up to the boss
LOUISE SOREL	My ass
BILL CULLEN	. . . My foot
BILL DAILY	She asked me first!
GENE RAYBURN	Dice
FRED GRANDY	. . . it and make it better
BETTY WHITE	Your lover
LOUISE SOREL	Men . . . women . . . whatever
BILL CULLEN	A rosary
ELAINE JOYCE	Goodnight
PETER MARSHALL	A lady's hand
DICK MARTIN	A handy lady
BRETT SOMERS	The Blarney Stone
CHARLES NELSON REILLY	The Pope's ring
BETTY WHITE	. . . and tell!

Things You Put in Your Mouth

Washington, D.C.   **A**rt Buchwald is a convivial curmudgeon and, in addition, a columnist, best-selling author, and just about everybody's idea of what a newspaperman is supposed to look like.

If there really is such a thing as reincarnation, and we get a choice, a whole lot of us are going to come back as Art Buchwald.

Hat in hand, I took the liberty of asking Mr. Buchwald and a number of our other celebrities whether they would each give me a single item in the category, THINGS YOU PUT IN YOUR MOUTH.

Score 5 points for each answer you can come up with and 10 points if you match any of our celebrities' wonderful but occasionally ridiculous bonus retorts. Food, drink, and musical instruments are off limits because of obvious space limitations!

Ed Asner

ART BUCHWALD	Mud pies and your foot
JIMMY BRESLIN	Cigars and pencils
JOANNA CASSIDY	Forks, spoons
JOYCE SELZNICK	Toothpicks
BETTY WHITE	You've got to be kidding
DICK VAN PATTEN	Toothpaste
ED ASNER	Dolly Parton

Bobby Vinton

Bill Cullen

Laurie Walters

TONY DANZA	Anything I can get
SLIM PICKENS	Chewin' tobacco
LAURIE WALTERS	Breath spray
DEAN JONES	Bubble gum
TONY ORLANDO	Braces
JAMES KOMACK	Straws
FRED GRANDY	Sunglasses
BEN VEREEN	Tongue depressers
BOBBY VINTON	Thermometer
TWIGGY	Thread
MARILU HENNER	Fingernails
JED ALLEN	Pacifier
GENE RAYBURN	Breasts
BILL CULLEN	Gold fillings
BRETT SOMERS	Whatever's available
MARILYN CHAMBERS	Strangers

Things That Go
In and Out

The phone rings at one of Beverly Hills' most exclusive hotels. Ellen Burstyn answers.

I ask her please to name some THINGS THAT GO IN AND OUT.

She doesn't hang up, which surprises me. Her responses are worth recording. They are presented here along with 26 other classics from our celebrities.

Take a bonus for each of your answers to this one: 3 points for anything you match from the celebrities' list, and 3 points for anything you think of that they didn't. (We're looking for things like the tide, or ball-point-pen tips . . .)

Marilu Henner

ELLEN BURSTYN	I have no idea
BETTY WHITE	Revolving doors
MARILU HENNER	One-night stands
BILL CULLEN	Groundhogs
PRISCILLA PRESLEY	Cuckoo birds
MADELINE KAHN	A turtle's head
THE DUKE OF BEDFORD	A maze
DEAN JONES	Entrances and exits
ANDREW BEST	Basketballs
BILL DAILY	Burt Reynolds

Dick Van Patten

ED ASNER	Soldiers of fortune
PATRICK TERRAIL	Switchblades
DICK VAN PATTEN	Tennis balls
LUCIE ARNAZ	Commuters
DONNA BEST	Your breath
CHARLES NELSON REILLY	The tide
ELLEN BURSTYN	Look, I'm really in a hurry . . .
TONY DANZA	Ball-point-pen tips
LAURIE WALTERS	A lizard's tongue
JOANNA CASSIDY	William F. Buckley's tongue
FRED GRANDY	Our daily bread
LOU RAWLS	Turnstiles
REGINE	Cigarette smoke
MORGAN FAIRCHILD	Advice goes in one ear and out the other!
SLIM PICKENS	Needles
CALVIN KLEIN	Fads
SIR FREDDIE LAKER	Tourists
JIMMY BRESLIN	The Holland Tunnel
MARILYN CHAMBERS	Vibrators
ELLEN BURSTYN	We're going to have to do this some other time

...AND MORE THINGS

Things You Find in the Kitchen Beginning with the Letter C

Regine

SEAN M. BYRNES

Patrick Terrail

With my customary perfect timing, I imposed upon the world-renowned hostess Regine, who owns and operates immensely successful discos and kitchens in Paris, the south of France, South America and New York, on what turned out to be the New York club's gala fifth anniversary. Some 650 glittering celebrity guests: Halston and Liza, of course Regine herself, making those of us who still need two names feel just slightly like a sophomore in a rented tux.

Later I asked the question of Ma Maison's Patrick Terrail, famed epicurian Craig Claiborne, and Elizabeth Schneider Colchie, contributing editor to "The International Review of Food and Wine" and co-author of *Better Than Store Bought.*

In addition, our celebrities have been aided here by a number of gifted former students of Le Cordon Bleu in Paris.

Feel free to use the names of particular foods or spices, if you wish. Our celebrities were asked to exclude the likes of "chicken" and "cabbage" so that they could move on to the more esoteric and exotic.

Take 1 point for each answer, and 2 points for those that made me smile (*).

* Cabinets (P.T.)
Caddy
* Cafe curtains (P.T.)
Cake dish
Cake knife
* Calendar (R.)
* Calories (E.S.C.)
Calorie counter
Calphalon Cookware
Candles (birthday)
Candy dish
Canisters
Can opener
Cans
Cappucino machine
Carafe
* Carnivores (C.C.)
Cart
Cast iron cookware
Carving knives
Case knife
* Casement windows
   (P.T.)
Casserole dish
* Cash (R.)
* Casters
Catsup bottle
Cauldron
* Caulking
* Ceiling (P.T.)
* Ceiling light (C.C.)

Centigrade
   thermometer
Cereal bowls
Chair
Chalice
Chalk
Chalkboard
* Change
Cheese board
Cheese slicer
Chef
Chest
* Children (P.T.)
Chimes (Front Door)
Chimney
* Cholesterol (C.C.)
Chop sticks
Chopping block
* Chrome
Churn
Clamp
Cleanser
Cleaver
Clock
Cloth
* Clutter (E.S.C.)
Coffee can
* Coffee klatches (E.S.C.)
Coffee cups
coffee filters

Coffee grinder
Coffee pot
* Cold spot (P.T.)
Colander
Comet
Condiments
Cook books
Cookie cutters
Cookie jar
Cookie sheet
Cooks
Cookstove
Cookware
Copper pots
Corkscrew
* Countertop (E.S.C.)
* Craig Claiborne (P.T.)
Creamer
* Creeping Charlie (R.)
Crepe pan
Crisper
Crockpot
Crystal
* Cubes (ice)
* Cuisinart (R.)
Cupboards
Cup hooks
Cups
Curtains
Cutting board

Things That Come in Pairs and Begin with the Letter B

San Fernando Valley
California

It is a searingly hot day in the Valley, but inside, in the lobby of Steve Allen's office, the air conditioner is on.

There are signs up all over the place, like "Have a Nice Day" and "This Thermostat is to Remain on at All Times." There are five signs on the subject of smoking: "Thank You for Not Smoking" and "No Smoking" and "No Smoking Anytime!" etc. There is also a very nice antique bench and the obligatory plant, parched and lonely, leaning longingly toward the towering green hedgerow across the street beyond the hermetically sealed room.

Without smoking or touching the thermometer, I asked Steve Allen, and eventually several of our other celebrities, to name some things that come in pairs and begin with the letter B, like bobby sox, or book ends.

Take 3 points for each answer you come up with. Don't peek at the celebrities' answers first!

Steve Allen

STEVE ALLEN	Badminton rackets
ED ASNER	Bisexuals
TONY DANZA	Boxers
BIANCA JAGGER	Bookends

Ben Vereen

Mort Sahl

JIMMY BRESLIN	Buddies
TONY ORLANDO	Binaural speakers
MARILU HENNER	Breasts
REX REED	Bifocals
BETTY WHITE	Bicycle wheels
BEN VEREEN	Biceps
LIBERACE	Bye-byes
DICK VAN PATTEN	Brides and grooms
JUDITH KRANTZ	Blue eyes
SHARI LEWIS	Boots
DAVID BRENNER	Backstrokes
PETER MARSHALL	Brackets
MILTON BERLE	Bus doors
JAMES KOMACK	Bowling shoes
JOEL GREY	Bongos
LUCIE ARNAZ	Blind dates
CALVIN KLEIN	Braids
BEN VEREEN	Blood brothers
JOYCE BROTHERS	Bobby sox
JIM LANGE	Bounderies
BILL CULLEN	Biplane wings
DICK MARTIN	Buns
FRED GRANDY	Bridge ends
ELIZABETH ASHLEY	Briefs
GENE RAYBURN	Bull's horns
RICHARD HATCH	Brakes
PRISCILLA PRESLEY	Bee's wings
MARILYN CHAMBERS	Bedposts
JOANNA CASSIDY	Barettes
MORT SAHL	Battery cables
DAVID NIVEN	Bedfellows
PETER USTINOV	Bird's feet

Things You Find in Bed That Begin with the Letter P

All right! Let's go back to that boisterous dressing room at CBS, now that the vino being drunk out of plastic glasses is almost gone. People are beginning to prepare for the next show, so there is a constant milling around of bodies through this room and the outer hall.

With only the slightest hesitation, I ask whether anyone would care to attempt the category of things you find in bed that begin with the letter P.

"With the letter P?" asks Brett quizzically.

"Yes."

"*Phucking!*" she shouts, pronouncing the letter P.

"Exactly what kind of interview is this?" Charles Nelson Reilly asks politely.

"Pajamas!" Dear Betty White brings everyone's attention to the question at hand.

"Who the hell still sleeps in pajamas?" someone in the corner wants to know.

"Pat Boone," comes the answer.

"Wait, wait!" Joyce Bulifant is waving her hand in the air as if she were in kindergarten. "I've got an answer for things you find in bed beginning with P— Pat Boone's pajamas!"

Betty White was made the honorary captain because without her we never would have made it through this one.

Elaine Joyce

Richard Deacon

Score 1 point for each acceptable answer and 2 points if you match one of our celebrity answers.

BETTY WHITE	Pajamas
CHARLES NELSON REILLY	Pajama parties
FRED GRANDY	Pinky Lee
BRETT SOMERS	Part-time work
PETER MARSHALL	Piecework
LOUISE SOREL	Peace offerings
BILL CULLEN	Percale sheets
IRA SKUTCH	Passion
DICK MARTIN	Perverts
CHARLES NELSON REILLY	Pseudonyms
RICHARD DEACON	Penises
ELAINE JOYCE	Paternity suits
BETTY WHITE	Pedal pushers
JOYCE BULIFANT	Phantasies
FRED GRANDY	Patent-leather pumps
CHARLES NELSON REILLY	Promiscuity
BETTY WHITE	Premarital sex
PETER MARSHALL	Premature ejaculation
BILL CULLEN	Prostitutes
GENE RAYBURN	Pimps
JAN GOUGH-GRANDY	Prudes
BRETT SOMERS	Prophylactics
CHARLES NELSON REILLY	Pornography
ELAINE JOYCE	Pillows
BILL CULLEN	Pillow talk
FRED GRANDY	Probation officers
IRA SKUTCH	Prurient interest
LOUISE SOREL	Playboy centerfolds
DICK MARTIN	Police dogs
RICHARD DEACON	Protestants

BETTY WHITE	The postman
JOYCE BULIFANT	Practice makes perfect
DICK MARTIN	Peroxide blondes
BILL DAILY	Patchwork quilts
BRETT SOMERS	Paratroopers
ELAINE JOYCE	Peignoirs
BILL DAILY	Pay dirt
GENE RAYBURN	Projection equipment
BILL DAILY	Puerto Ricans
FRED GRANDY	Pharmaceutical aids
IRA SKUTCH	Pot
BILL DAILY	Little plastic things with batteries
LOUISE SOREL	The Pittsburgh Steelers
BRETT SOMERS	Paul Newman
DICK MARTIN	Paul Williams
FRED GRANDY	Peter, Paul and Mary
BILL CULLEN	Prostate trouble
JAN GOUGH-GRANDY	Porthault linen
PETER MARSHALL	Prayer
BETTY WHITE	Propositions
ELAINE JOYCE	Primitive instincts
BILL DAILEY	Poultry
CHARLES NELSON REILLY	Peccadillos
FRED GRANDY	Picadors
BRETT SOMERS	Pickets
JAN GOUGH-GRANDY	Proposals
RICHARD DEACON	Prevention
JOYCE BULIFANT	Positions
ELAINE JOYCE	Procurers
CHARLES NELSON REILLY	Pom-pom girls
BILL DAILY	Pristine
FRED GRANDY	Pick ups
BETTY WHITE	Puckers

Joyce Bulifant

49

Bill Daily

PETER MARSHALL	Perfume and pinching
ELAINE JOYCE	Pillow cases
LOUISE SOREL	Panty raids
DICK MARTIN	Panties
BILL DAILY	Panting
BETTY WHITE	Passivity
IRA SKUTCH	Poets
FRED GRANDY	Pogo sticks
GENE RAYBURN	Polygamy
JOYCE BULIFANT	Pads, like on a mattress
CHARLES NELSON REILLY	Pads, like in Joyce's bra
PETER MARSHALL	Petting
BETTY WHITE	Pets
ELAINE JOYCE	Powder and perfume
BILL CULLEN	Philanderers
IRA SKUTCH	Penetration
LOUISE SOREL	Pests
BRETT SOMERS	Phonies
FRED GRANDY	Plague victims
CHARLES NELSON REILLY	Polaroids and promises

Things You Wear That Begin with the Letter S

London   **L**ess than an hour ago, Calvin Klein invited us to the gala South Molton Street opening of his new shop. Mr. Klein designs for all the senses. The air is rich with dark wool tweed, lambswool, and angora. Only half hearing what Calvin is saying, I mentally race through potential categories until I find one that seems to work. Let's see, "suits . . . shirts . . . sarongs . . ." yes, there should be plenty of possible answers to this one.

"Calvin," I interrupt, "I'd like you to think of the letter S."

Calvin nods.

"Beginning with the letter S, can you name 30 THINGS YOU WEAR?"

Calvin frowns. "Things you wear?"

"Yes."

"With an S?"

"Yes." I'm getting worried now. Perhaps 30 is too many. Should I have asked for 20?

"Thirty things you wear, beginning with S," he says, almost whispering. That famous face is beginning to curl now into an impish grin.

Calvin Klein gave me my 30 answers. I could probably have asked for 40, or 50 for that matter. And not once did he mention suits or shirts or sarongs.

List as many answers as you can, and don't stop at 30;
try to out-think Calvin Klein. You get a point for
everything you can think of that fits the category, and
5 points for anything you match from Calvin's list.
Then, we'll take a look at a list of answers provided
by a very talented group of students at New York's
Parsons School of Design.

CALVIN'S LIST

Sizes	Skin	Scarlet ribbons
Small	Skins	Silver
Silk	Sackcloth and ashes	Swiss watches
Satin	Shoelaces	Sapphires
Sable	Shoulder holster	A sling
Seersucker	Schiaparelli	A splint
A smile	Skis	Your Sunday best
Scents	String of pearls	Supporter
Sunglasses	Spats	Skullcap
A scowl	Spurs	Star of David

PARSONS SCHOOL OF DESIGN LIST

Single breasted coat	Sweatsuit	Snowshoes
Sweater	Skirt	Skis
Sleeveless sweater	Sportcoat	A shiner
Shirtwaist	Smoking jacket	Shin guards
Shorts	Shoes	A sneer
Swimsuit	Socks	Sheath
Sack dress	Stockings	Surcoat
Sarong	Sabatos	Sheepskin
Slacks	Sandals	Suntan lotion
Sweatshirt	Slippers	Sweatband

Ski mask
Sleep mask
Smock
Shako
Sallet
Scarf
Shades
Swim fins
Sun bonnet

Sun dress
Slip
Swaddling cloth
Sash
Snakeskin
Shroud
Sergeant stripes
Sailor suit
Shoulder pads

Sleeves
Stretch pants
Strapless bra
Strapless gown
Sari
Stickpin
Slave bracelets
Side arms

Things That Keep You Up At Night that Begin with the Letter C

Las Vegas I'm talking to David Brenner one night after his act; his adrenalin is still pumping, the laughter is still alive in his ears.

"Ask me something," he insists.

"Relax, we'll do it later."

"Oh, sure! You tell me all about Woody Allen's great answers and how terrific Ben Vereen was, and then you won't ask me one lousy question!"

"I don't ask lousy questions."

"Then ask me a great question."

"I'll ask you a serious question."

"All right, I'll give you a serious answer."

"No you won't!"

"You're right!"

"David, if you could go back into your past, who is the one person you'd like to see again?"

"Mr. Johnson!"

The room is quiet now. Michael's camera stops clicking, waiting for the other shoe to drop. David's road manager, Steve Reidman, turns to me and shrugs. David's going to make us ask.

"Do you want to tell me who Mr. Johnson is?"

"No."

"Then, tell me something you wouldn't want to touch."

"Tricia Nixon, boiling water, and New Jersey!"

David Brenner

54

"Those are Woody Allen answers!"

"Oh great! You come in here and ask me an old, used, Woody Allen question, after all the good answers have already been taken!"

"All right. I'll ask you a brand new question I haven't asked anybody else. What is your favorite sound?"

"Fat people walking! Actually, that's my least favorite sound. My favorite sound is Jacqueline Bisset sleeping next to me! Another sound that I don't like is conventioneers. I don't like any sound that anybody makes at a convention."

"Can you give me a couple of famous names that you can eat or drink? Names like Jack Lemmon or James Bacon."

"Jacqueline Bisset!"

"What's a bisset?"

"Make something up, call it a bisset, I'll eat it!"

"Can you tell me something that it's impossible to do alone?"

"Tennis! You can, but it's stupid!"

"Tell me something that you wouldn't want to touch."

"This question!"

"Tell me something that you really wouldn't want to touch."

"Doc Severinson . . . a live barracuda's tooth . . . Sonny Scungilli . . . Bella Abzug, Tricia Nixon, boiling water, and New Jersey!"

In the course of our conversation David and I discover that we both sleep only about 4 hours a night. The reason I sleep so little is that I like the glare of neon on the empty city streets at night, or maybe it's nervous tension. For David, sleeping so little is something he taught himself to do.

When he was a kid in South Philadelphia, David noticed an old Italian guy who was always still awake when David went to sleep and was already awake when he woke up again the next day. David took a piece of paper and figured out that that old guy was going to live twice as long as anybody else—if living is being awake and knowing what is going on around you. For the next two years, David Brenner changed his sleep pattern, cutting his sleeping time by 5 minutes every week, until he could function on only 4 hours of sleep in 24.

If you sleep 4 hours a night and I sleep 8, you are awake 28 hours more than I am each week. That adds up to a day and 4 hours extra per week, or 4 days and 16 hours per month. Eight weeks a year!

For David Brenner, the year is 60 weeks long. Fourteen months. He's now 4 years, 6 months, and 9 hours older than the kids he went to school with. You can eat a lot of pizzas and chase a lot of skirts in 5 years. Of course that also means that by the time he's 65, he'll have "lived" 74 years, 9 months, and some odd hours—and probably be too tired to remember what you're supposed to do with a Bisset or a pepperoni pizza. I asked the yawning and aging Mr. Brenner whether he could name some THINGS THAT KEEP YOU UP AT NIGHT AND BEGIN WITH THE LETTER C.

Take 2 points for each answer and an extra 5 points for anything that matches one of David's.

Carson	Counting sheep	Cymbals
Cats	Camping out	Cupid
Cat burglars	Calls	Coffee
Celibacy	Consummating your	Caffeine
Crybabies	marriage	Cannibals
Cyclones	Charo	Cruising
Cat fights	Catnaps	Creaking floorboards

56

Colds
Catastrophies
Comanches
Cunnilingus
Celebrating New Year's
    Eve
Constipation
Critics
Your conscience
Curry powder

Culpability
Counterrevolution
Coronary
Copulating
Conventions
A commotion
Coitus
Breaking the
    commandments
Childbirth

Conga dancers
Cantilevered houses
Cleavage
Clatter
Call girls
Complaints
A cockfight
Calliopes
Cod liver oil
Cannon fire

Things You Wouldn't Want in Your Sleeping Bag that Begin with the Letter C

George Carlin is the kind of man who notices that "fat chance" and "slim chance" mean exactly the same thing. Attempting to interview George on a New York street corner one afternoon, we drew quite a crowd I suggested collecting a quarter from everyone who wanted to watch. We made $2.75.

I asked one of the onlookers to select a letter, and he chose C. So using the letter C, give us as many THINGS YOU WOULDN'T WANT TO FIND IN YOUR SLEEPING BAG THAT BEGIN WITH THE LETTER C as you can think of. If you are playing alone, see how many you can get in five minutes. If you are in a team, each player has to think up an answer within 10 seconds of the previous answer. Score 3 points for each correct answer.

GEORGE CARLIN Charles Bronson, crabs, and cream of chicken soup!

DAVID BRENNER Comanches!

BEN VEREEN Cockroaches.

MIKE DOUGLAS Cannibals!

REX REED Cholera!

JOEL GREY   Crocodiles.

MORGAN FAIRCHILD   Count Dracula.

PETER USTINOV   A cadaver.

STEVE ALLEN   A crazy person.

ED ASNER   Minnie Pearl!

RAY REESE   With the letter C!

ED ASNER   Ca-Ca!

JIMMY BRESLIN   Carbon monoxide.

MARILU HENNER   "Candid Camera"!

MADELINE KAHN   Typhoid Mary!

JED ALLEN   Casanova.

PETER MARSHALL   Che Che Rodriguez!

VERNON JORDAN   Cactus.

JUDITH KRANTZ   Cobras.

TONY DANZA   Caterpillars.

DR. JOYCE BROTHERS   Cold feet.

BETTY WHITE   The CIA.

DICK VAN PATTEN   A cyclone.

ALTOVISE DAVIS   Charo!

DAVID BRENNER   A convention!

REGINE   Cotton candy.

TONY ORLANDO   Celibacy.

GEORGE BURNS   Carrie Nation!

DAVID BRENNER   The cantor's daughter!
Cossacks! Don Corleone's wife! Candy apples! Cardinal
Cushing!

Tony Orlando

59

Ray Reese

MILTON BERLE   Chicken à la king.

DAVID BRENNER   Camp Fire girls!

SAMMY DAVIS, JR.   Cherries Jubilee.

RAY REESE   Time's up!

DAVID BRENNER   A contagious disease.
Cowboys! A cockfight! A Czechoslovakian virgin!
Crochet hooks. Catholics!

INITIALS ...

H.H.

Knowing how she loves people who pose totally innocuous questions, I asked Helene Hanff, the author of *84 Charing Cross Road,* how many people she could name who share her initials, H.H.

Helene and Lucie Arnaz both put on their thinking caps and they came up with 25 H.H.'s, two special bonus H.H.H.'s, and one answer with identical first and last names.

Score 4 points for each correct answer and 10 points for the bonuses. Happy hunting!

Huntz Hall
Hannibal Hamlin
Harold Happy
   Harston**
Huntington Hartford
Hurd Hatfield
Henry Hathaway
Howard Hawks
Helen Hayes

Hermann Hesse
Howard Hesseman
Henry Higgins*
Harriet Hilliard
Heinrich Himmler
Hal Holbrook
Hot Lips Hoolihan
Herbert Hoover
Hedda Hopper

Horatio Hornblower
Harry Houdini
Huckleberry Hound
Howard Hughes
Henry Hull
Humbert Humbert**
Hubert Horatio
   Humphrey**
H. L. Hunt

A. K. A.

The Plaza Hotel
New York

I never knew there were so many beautiful people in the world. It can be disorienting to spend the morning watching Francesco Scavullo focus his camera on the face and figure that will eventually grace the cover of next month's *Cosmopolitan* magazine, the afternoon face to face with Richard Chamberlain, and the evening with Maude Adams or Lauren Hutton right there, warm and breathing in front of you.

Thank god for Jimmy Breslin! I called him at home this morning and he said—perfectly synchronized with the tempo of his typewriter clicking away in the background—"Yeah . . . sure . . . we'll set a meeting . . . I'll buy you a cup of coffee." That's how Jimmy Breslin is. If he likes you, all you have to do is ask. If he doesn't like you? Ask him anyway—he hates to say no.

Jimmy Breslin is what's left of "Hildy" from *The Front Page*. Doubly cursed, with a reporter's nose and a poet's tongue, Jimmy is the kind of guy Dashiell Hammett would have liked. In this age of computer-typeset single-edition newspapers and television personalities on the news who call themselves reporters, Jimmy should get tenure at Columbia. Having met most of those who grace the covers of most magazines these days, I would stand up if Eleanor Roosevelt or Satchel Paige or Jimmy Breslin entered the room, but that's about it. Jimmy has a way with words. If you want to find out what's going in that White House office that H. R. Haldeman used to think was his ("Nothin'!") or where to find the best cup of coffee in New York ("the Chambers Coffee Shop, at Sixth Avenue and Fifty-ninth Street—but you have to ask for Angie"), just ask Jimmy.

Psst! Don't look around, but Eddie "Two Fingers" just walked in wit' Tony "The Weasel." And if you hadn't already guessed, this time we're looking for people who are known by nicknames, like Baby Face Nelson, or The Bard. The celebrity team boasts a few nicknames of its own, as well as some unfortunates who still use the name they were born with: Sugar Ray Leonard, Slim Pickens, Jimmy Breslin, Ed Asner, Kurt Russell, David Brenner, Dick Van Patten, and Tony Danza.

Score 1 point for each famous nickname you can think of.

Cannonball Adderley (Julian Adderley)

The Greatest (Muhammad Ali)

Billy "White Shoes" Anderson; Bronco Billy Anderson

Fatty Arbuckle

Satchmo (Louis Armstrong)

The Tennessee Plowboy (Eddy Arnold)

The Singing Cowboy (Gene Autry)

Baby; Slim (Lauren Bacall)

The Profile (John Barrymore)

Tex Benecke

Mr. Television (Milton Berle)

The Divine Sarah (Sarah Bernhardt)

The Little Corporal (Napoleon Bonaparte)

The Angelic Assassin; The Swedish Undertaker (Bjorn Borg)

Diamond Jim Brady

The Wild Bull of the Pampas (Primo Carnera)

Wilt "The Stilt" Chamberlain

Chubby Checker

Buffalo Bill Cody

Gentleman Jim Corbett

Douglas "Wrong Way" Corrigan

Buster Crabbe

Der Bingle (Bing Crosby)

Benjamin "Scatman" Crothers
Man Mountain Dean
The Manassa Mauler (Jack Dempsey)
Fats Domino
The Schnoz (Jimmy Durante)
Leo "The Lip" Durocher
Mister B. (Billy Eckstein)
The Wizard of Menlo Park (Thomas Alva Edison)
Skinny Ennis
Dr. J. (Julius Erving)
Pretty Boy Floyd
Tennessee Ernie Ford
Whitey Ford
Fearless Fosdick
Redd Foxx
Smokin' Joe Frazier
The King (Clark Gable)
Two-Ton Tony Galento
The Iron Man (Lou Gehrig)
Hoot Gibson
Dizzy Gillespie
King of Swing (Benny Goodman)
Mean Joe Green
Richard "Racehorse" Haines
Gabby Hayes (George Hayes)
Elroy "Crazylegs" Hirsh
Wild Bill Hickok

Lady Day (Billie Holliday)
Ski Nose (Bob Hope)
Jim "Catfish" Hunter
Ivory Joe Hunter
Illinois Jacket
Henry "Scoop" Jackson
Erwin "Magic" Johnson
Ed "Too Tall" Jones
Stone Face (Buster Keaton)
Machine Gun Kelly
Lawrence of Arabia (T. E. Lawrence)
Irving "Swifty" Lazar
Sugar Ray Leonard
Honest Abe; The Rail Splitter (Abraham Lincoln)
The Swedish Nightingale (Jenny Lind)
Lucky Lindy (Charles Lindbergh)
The Bear (Sonny Liston)
The Brown Bomber (Joe Louis)
Lucky Luciano
Bugsy Malone
Pistol Pete Maravich
The Brockton Bomber (Rocky Marciano)
The Swamp Fox (Francis Marion)
Chico, Groucho, Gummo, Harpo, and Zeppo Marx (The Marx Brothers)

The Divine Miss M. (Bette Midler)
Bugs Moran
Stan "The Man" Musial
Il Duce (Benito Mussolini)
Broadway Joe Namath
Baby Face Nelson
Red Norvo
Leroy "Satchel" Paige
Charlie "Bird" Parker
Blood and Guts (General George Patton)
Slim Pickens
Bebe Rebozo
Pee Wee Reese
James "Scotty" Reston
The Red Baron (Manfred von Richthofen)
Tex Ritter
Eddie "Bojangles" Robinson
Sugar Ray Robinson
Rocky (Nelson Rockefeller)
Che Che Rodriguez
King of the Cowboys (Roy Rogers)
The Desert Fox (Field Marshall Erwin Rommel)
Slapsy Maxie Rosenbloom
Babe Ruth; The Sultan of Swat (George Herman Ruth)
Bugsy Seigal

The Bard (William
   Shakespeare)
Neil "Doc" Simon
Chairman of the Board;
   Old Blue Eyes (Frank
   Sinatra)
Red Skelton
Bubba Smith
Jimmy the Greek
   (Jimmy Snyder)
Silkie Sullivan

Arthur "Punch"
   Sulzberger
The Assassin (Jack
   Tatum)
The Saint (Simon
   Templar)
The Motor City Cobra
   (Thomas Hearns)
The Sheik (Rudolph
   Valentino)

Vlad the Impaler
Fats Waller
The Duke (John Wayne)
Slappy White
Tennessee Williams
   (Thomas Lanier
   Williams)
Tex Williams
Wolfman Jack
Mighty Joe Young

C.C.

There are comedians, and there are comics, and comedic actors, but there are almost no court jesters anymore. For one thing, very few have the face and body for the costume: the floppy-pointed hat and the boots with bells on the tips of curled toes. The next time you open up a brand new deck of playing cards, take a look and see for yourself. Charlie Callas is a jester. A man who performs as if a standing ovation or the guillotine at dawn were his only options.

In homage to Charlie, I asked him to think of all the famous people who have the initials C.C. You are invited to try your hand, too. You get 2 points for each name on Charlie's list, and 3 points for each name you think of that Charlie didn't.

Cab Calloway
Calvin Coolidge
Candy Clark
Cardinal Cushing
Carlos Castenada
Carmen Cavallero
Carol Channing
Carol Cooke

Carrie Chapman Catt
Cassius Clay
Clark Clifford
Cesar Chavez
Charles Chaplin
Charles Coburn
Charles Collingwood
Charlie Callas

Charlie Chan
Cheech & Chong *
Chester A. Conklin
Chevy Chase
Christopher Columbus
Christopher Craft
Christopher Cross
Chick Correa

Chuck Conners
Chubby Checker
Claudette Colbert
Claudia Cardinale
Clive Cussler

Coco Chanel
Connie Chung
Constance Cummings
Corinne Calvet
Craig Claiborne

Curtis Cokes
Cyd Charisse
Cy Coleman
Chris Connelly

People Who Have
The Initials J.C.

What is the first name that comes to mind when you think of the initials J.C.? That's the question I shouted over the heads of the Secret Service men as Former President Jimmy Carter was led into a fund-raising benefit at the Century Plaza Hotel in Los Angeles. Without missing a beat he flashed me that infamous smile and gave me his answer.

Ted Kennedy paused for a moment on his way into the ABC television studios, considered the obvious, and then rejected it, providing us with an intriguing bonus answer. When he heard the question, Ronald Reagan laughed out loud.

The responses of 12 celebrities, including a liberal sprinkling of politicians, are listed on the next page. But before you peek at them, see how many famous J.C.'s you can think of. Then take a crack at matching President Reagan, Senator Kennedy, Jimmy Carter, and the other celebrities to their responses.

Score 3 points for each of your own J.C.'s and 5 points each time you match a celebrity to his or her answer. If you figure out which one is Senator Kennedy's, take a bow—and a 10-point bonus.

Here's what the celebrities said when asked to name someone with the initials J.C. Match each response below to the celebrity who said it. Answers are at the bottom of the page.

Jimmy Carter   Ted Kennedy
Dick Van Patten   Ruth Gordon
Marilyn Chambers   Mike Douglas
Ronald Reagan   Moshe Dayan
Steve Allen   Madeline Kahn
Ben Vereen   Peter Ustinov

1. Jesus Christ_____
2. Johnny Carson_____
3. Julie Christie_____
4. Jimmy Carter_____
5. Johnny Cash_____
6. Jimmy Cagney_____
7. John Chancellor_____
8. Julius Caesar_____
9. Jimmy Caan_____
10. Jacques Cousteau_____
11. Jill Clayburgh_____
12. Jiminy Cricket_____

...AND NAMES

Tinker, Tailor

Lucie Arnaz was the very first person we interviewed for this book. The interview was accomplished in bits and pieces: in person, on the phone, and by means of hastily scribbled letters and notes. When we first contacted Lucie and she agreed to be interviewed, she was in the middle of closing in her long-running Broadway hit, *They're Playing Our Song,* rehearsing for a new play, getting married to Laurence Luckinbill, and planning her honeymoon. She found the time anyway.

I learned a lot during that first interview. For instance, I found that if I would simply keep my mouth shut, celebrities will often tell you a whole lot more than you ever hoped or expected to hear.

We asked Lucie how many famous people she could think of who have names that are occupations, like Ava Gardner and Howard Baker. Lucie thought of tons of such names, including first-name candidates. You may not want to do this all in one sitting, because answers are going to be popping into your head at the strangest times for days to come. Be prepared to climb out of the shower and get your paper soaking wet as you scribble down something thoroughly brilliant that just occurred to you.

Score 1 point per answer, 2 points for bonuses (*), and 5 points for special bonuses (**).

Josephine Baker
Red Barber
Ma Barker
Joey Bishop
Booker T. Washington *
Teresa Brewer *
Rhett Butler
Eddie Cantor *
Liz Carpenter
Hoss Cartwright *
John Chancellor *
Alistair Cooke
Alice Cooper
Deacon Jones
James Dean
Doc Severinson
Patty Duke
Earl "Fatha" Hines
Fannie Farmer
Carrie Fisher
George Foreman *
Maureen Forrester
Randy Gardiner

Ava Gardner
Vittorio Gassman *
Barbara Goldsmith
Eydie Gorme
Billy Joe Hooker *
John Houseman
Tab Hunter
Stephen King
Harvey Korman *
Jack Lord
Penny Marshall
James Mason
Louis B. Mayer *
Adrian Messenger *
Henry Miller
Georgia Moll *
Thelonius Monk *
Gail Parent *
Estelle Parsons
Pontius Pilate *
Christopher Plummer
Joan Plowright

Carmelita Pope *
Ivy Baker Priest **
Hal Prince
Victoria Principal *
Richard Pryor
Sargent Shriver
John Singer Sargent **
Katie Saylor
Peter Sellers
Alan Shepard
Robert Sherriff
Willie Shoemaker
Jaclyn Smith
Justice Potter Stewart **
Roscoe Tanner
Taylor Caldwell
James Taylor
Edward Teller *
Margaret Thatcher
Grant Tinker *
Porter Waggoner **
Dennis Weaver

People Known by Two
First Names

Monaco   It is 7:23 in the magic Monte Carlo evening, and I am seated amid the ornate oak paneled ambiance of the bar at the Hotel de Paris, waiting for Orson Welles.

At a nearby table, Count Don Juan de Bourbon, past pretender to the throne of Spain and father of the present King, is explaining to David Niven why he is never going to play another game of golf. I feel wonderful, this is where I was meant to be!

Suddenly the massive carved oak doors at the far end of the luxurious room swing open unaided, and Orson Welles enters.

Even here, an audible tremor ripples through the room at the sight of him. I rise as he moves to join me, thinking of how envious they all must be. Mr. Welles sweeps past my table to exchange pleasantries with Mr. Niven and his guest. I sit down. Finally, he returns to my table.

When he is seated, I notice for the first time that he is not alone. His entourage includes an astrologer and an exquisite sun-touched girl whom Orson refers to either as Claudia or Ethel. She answers to both names. Mr. Welles has that effect on people.

Complicated introductions are made in three languages.

With just the slightest rise of an impressive eyebrow, Orson inspects what we are drinking, has the crystal glasses removed with a majestic wave of his hand, and reorders for us.

Slowly I become aware that a massive silence has settled on the room. Orson fastens the entire table with a commanding stare. The entire table turns to stare at me. Orson does the same.

Feeling foolish, the way one must have felt in the sudden presence of a Tudor king, I try to explain to the maker of *Citizen Kane* that I would like him to take a little test!

Mr. Welles is smiling, waiting patiently. Ethel is busying herself filing an errant nail. The wine arrives for Mr. Welles's approval, and I still have not uttered an intelligible word.

Just as I am about to gain a firm foothold on what I am about to say, we are joined by Mr. Niven and the Count and the complicated introductions begin again.

Raising his glass, Mr. Welles proposes a toast ". . . to absent friends!" which I interpret into Italian for the perplexed astrologer. Mr. Welles nods and inquires, in a classic Venetian dialect that puts my stumbling Calabrian mutterings to shame, what sort of book it is that I'm doing.

Figuring I might as well get it over with, I explain, after only a few false starts, that we are looking for famous people known by two first names.

Orson's eyes are closed. "Like Ann-Margret?" he asks, opening one of them.

I hadn't thought of that one. "Well . . . yes, but I was thinking more of people with a first name and a last name that is commonly used as a first name. Like Steve Martin, or Peggy Lee."

"Ah, yes. Janis Ian, Victor Hugo, Dick Tracy, James Joyce," he says, closing the famous eye again.

The game has begun. To the delight of the surrounding tables, Mr. Welles taps his ivory-handled cane by way of punctuation as he rattles off his answers. Soon he stops and opens his massive eyes, his face breaking into a crinkling smile, as if to say that he could continue indefinitely, if we had the time. In just under four minutes, he has come up with an incredible 105 correct answers.

Before Orson was through he surprised us with not one but seven famous people known by three first names—and one famous French Lady who had four.

Give yourself 1 point for each name you think of, 10 points for each person known by three first names, and a whopping 25 points if you think of the French *dame* with four first names.

Henry Aaron	Stephen Douglas	Bob Hope
Ethan Allen	Bob Dylan	Leslie Howard
Fred Allen	Nelson Eddy	Trevor Howard
Gracie Allen	Cass Elliot	Victor Hugo
Steve Allen	Arlene Francis	Janis Ian
Mark Antony	Connie Francis	Amy Irving
Benedict Arnold	Anne Frank	Harry James
Eddie Arnold	Aretha Franklin	Henry James
Jack Benny	Benjamin Franklin	William James
Richard Benjamin	Crystal Gayle	Elton John
Tony Bill	Ruth Gordon	James Joyce
John Calvin	Billy Graham	Emmett Kelly
Diahann Carroll	Kate Graham	Gene Kelly
Ray Charles	Sheila Graham	Grace Kelly
Dick Clark	Virginia Graham	Clark Kent
Petula Clark	Cary Grant	Russell Kirk
Roy Clark	Lee Grant	Peggy Lee
Tony Curtis	Lou Grant	Janet Leigh
James Dean	Dick Gregory	Jerry Lewis
Sandy Dennis	James Gregory	Shari Lewis
Kirk Douglas	Laurence Harvey	Abraham Lincoln
Michael Douglas	Patrick Henry	Martin Luther

Loretta Lynn
Dean Martin
Mary Martin
Steve Martin
Lee Marvin
John Mitchell
Martha Mitchell
Thomas Mitchell
Wayne Morris
Anne Murray
Bill Murray
Willie Nelson
Martha Raye

Billy Rose
David Rose
Betsy Ross
Diana Ross
Jack Ruby
Bertrand Russell
Bill Russell
Kurt Russell
Carly Simon
John Simon
Neil Simon
Paul Simon

Sirhan Sirhan
James Stewart
Rod Stewart
Dylan Thomas
Lowell Thomas
Mike Todd
Dick Tracy
Spencer Tracy
George Wallace
Irving Wallace
Mike Wallace
John Wayne

Here are the seven three-name answers Orson came up with:

Hubert Horatio
   Humphrey
David Clayton-Thomas
Jerry Lee Lewis

James Earl Ray
Lee Harvey Oswald
Jamie Lee Curtis

And here, for 25 points, is the French lady known by four first names:

Josephine Jeanne Marie Antoinette

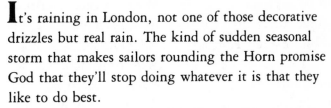

People Who Are Known by Three Names

It's raining in London, not one of those decorative drizzles but real rain. The kind of sudden seasonal storm that makes sailors rounding the Horn promise God that they'll stop doing whatever it is that they like to do best.

It doesn't rain on Judith Krantz. That's the first thing I noticed. That's what happens when you're Number One on the *New York Times* bestseller list.

Judith Krantz writes books that everybody reads. I approve. I approve of almost anybody who makes more money than me without using a gun or a guitar. Especially if they do it with a typewriter.

Ms. Krantz, along with Peter Ustinov, Ed Asner, and Jimmy Breslin, gave us some famous people who are known by three names.

Each answer is worth 1 point, and you get an extra 2 points if you guess the special bonus name(**), not human, provided by Peter Ustinov.

Peter Ustinov

John Quincy Adams
Hans Christian Andersen
John Jacob Astor
Johann Sebastian Bach
Stephen Vincent Benet
Thomas Hart Benton

Shirley Temple Black
John Wilkes Booth
Jorge Luis Borges
Helen Gurley Brown
Elizabeth Barrett
    Browning

James Branch Cabell
Jesus Lopez Cabos
George Washington
    Carver
June Carter Cash
James Fenimore Cooper

Francis Ford Coppola
Helen Gahagan Douglas
Arthur Conan Doyle
Ford Maddox Ford
John Kenneth Galbraith
David Lloyd George
Linda Day George
Paul Michael Glaser
William Randolph
  Hearst
Gil Scott Heron
George Roy Hill
Edward Everett Horton
John Paul Jones
James Earl Jones
Martin Luther King

John Phillip Law
Gypsy Rose Lee
Alan Jay Lerner
Jerry Lee Lewis
Anne Morrow Lindbergh
Henry Cabot Lodge
Henry Wadsworth
  Longfellow
James Russell Lowell
Claire Booth Luce
Mary Margaret McBride
Aimee Semple
  McPherson
Mary Ann Mobley
Mary Tyler Moore
Daniel Patrick Moynihan

Lee Harvey Oswald
Edgar Allan Poe
James Earl Ray
Charles Nelson Reilly
George Lincoln Rockwell
Franklin Delano
  Roosevelt
George Bernard Shaw
Wallis Warfield Simpson
Margaret Chase Smith
Harriet Beecher Stowe
John Cameron Swayze
John Clayton Thomas
Robert Penn Warren
Frank Lloyd Wright
Jesse Colin Young

And the nonhuman
  bonus name . . .

Rin Tin Tin**

People With Names You Can Eat or Drink

Ma Maison
Beverly Hills

If you are anywhere west of the Seine and you haven't had dinner yet, it's nice to know Patrick Terrail. Patrick is the owner of and genius behind Ma Maison, the successful restaurant "almost" in Beverly Hills—a restaurant so exclusive it has an unlisted telephone number. It's been said that you need to know only two people out on the Coast, Patrick Terrail and Irving "Swifty" Lazar, Patrick because he can get you a table at Ma Maison, and Irving because he can get you anything else!

This category was suggested impromptu by Patrick, allowing me to play along. Joining us were my good friend Jed Allen, who stars as Don Craig in "Days of Our Lives," comedian and wine connoisseur Dick Martin, Craig Claiborne, the food editor for the *New York Times,* and, thanks to Patrick, the exquisite Morgan Fairchild.

Webster's dictionary defines *gastronome* as "one who enjoys and has a discriminating taste for foods; an expert in all phases of the art and science of good eating." It would be difficult to find two more dedicated practitioners of the art than Patrick Terrail and Craig Claiborne. Certainly Wolfgang Puck, the world-famous chef at Ma Maison, fulfills the requirements, he interrupted late in the round with several incomparable contributions. Altogether, between the laughing and the crying, we came up with 60 acceptable answers. See how many you can think of.

Score 1 point for each answer, 3 points for bonuses(*), and 5 points for superbonuses(**).

PATRICK TERRAIL	Buster Crabbe
CRAIG CLAIBORNE	Sir Francis Bacon
JED ALLEN	Chuck Mangione*
MORGAN FAIRCHILD	Geoffrey Beene
RAY REESE	Coco Chanel
PATRICK	Donald Duck
CRAIG	David Lean
MORGAN	Fats Domino
RAY	Jack Lemmon
PATRICK	Ginger Rogers
CRAIG	Art Pepper
JED	Waldo Salt
MORGAN	Basil Rathbone
RAY	Margaret Mead
DICK	Sheree North
PATRICK	Curtis Cokes
DICK	Jellyroll Morton*
CRAIG	Anthony Quayle
MORGAN	Andrew Mellon
RAY	Albert Broccoli
DICK	Chief Justice Warren Burger
CRAIG	Bud Shank
JED	Dr. Pepper*
MORGAN	Michael Caine
DICK	Peanuts
WOLFGANG PUCK	Olive Oyl**
	Porky Pig**

Patrick Terrail

84

Ray Reese

DICK	Shirley Temple*
WOLFGANG	Jack Daniels*
DICK	The Gallo Brothers*
PATRICK	Paul Masson*
MORGAN	Peter Lemongello*
JED	Robert Crumb
RAY	Elizabeth Beveridge
DICK	The Earl of Sandwich*
PATRICK	Soupy Sales
CRAIG	William of Orange
MORGAN	O.J. Simpson*
RAY	Joseph Papp*
WOLFGANG	Punch and Judy
DICK	Don Juan de Bourbon
CRAIG	Barbara Hershey
JED	Candy Barr
RAY	Mandy Rice Davies
PATRICK	Edgar Rice Burroughs
MORGAN	Peaches and Herb
PATRICK	Hamilton Fish
CRAIG	Charles Lamb
WOLFGANG	Eddie Rabbitt
JED	Warren Oates
DICK	Baron de Rothschild
CRAIG	Sir Alec Guinness
WOLFGANG	Captain Beefheart
RAY	Bernard Buffet
DICK	Justice Felix Frankfurter
WOLFGANG	Gene Shalit
	Berry Berenson
	Chicken George
	The Partridge Family

Famous Names That Are Also Places

All right, you are about to find out what it's like to be Gulfport, Mississippi during the hurricane season! This is Rex Reed and Peter Ustinov that you're about to challenge. You're going to lose this one, I promise you!

The premise of this game is simple: we are looking for famous names that contain place names, like John Denver, or Julie London. Don't worry about spelling—as long as it sounds OK, the spelling doesn't have to be OK.

If you are starting to feel sorry for yourself, wait until I tell you the combined score of Mr. Ustinov and Mr. Reed: 137. But the really bad news is, you get only 1 point for each answer. But there are 5 bonus answers, each one worth 10 points—these are names where the first and last names are both place names.

Before you begin, fix yourself a pot of coffee, get the cold compress ready, and call a friend.

Peter Ustinov

Alberta Hunter
Morey Amsterdam
Pamela Austin
Steve Austin
Frankie Avalon

Irving Berlin
Tokyo Rose
Dr. Bombay
Maxine Cheshire
Chevy Chase

China Lee
Cleveland Amory
Christopher Columbus
Stella Dallas
Bob Denver

John Denver
Denver Pyle
Nathan Detroit
Morgan Britanny
Buffalo Bill Cody
Luther Burbank
Godfrey Cambridge
Little Egypt
Chad Everett
Douglas Fairbanks
Donna Fargo
Anatole France
France Nuyen
Florence Henderson
Florida Freibus
Joe Frisco
Georgia Brown
Georgia Gibbs
Georgia O'Keefe
Christina Holland
Thelma Houston
John Huston
Walter Huston
Jill Ireland

John Ireland
Washington Irving*
Jersey Joe Walcott
Scoop Jackson
Janis Joplin
Richard Jordan
Vernon Jordan
Ken McCord
Robert Lansing
Abraham Lincoln
Jack London
Julie London
Victoria De Los
    Angeles*
Melissa Manchester
Virginia Mayo*
Eddie Mekka
Monty Montana
Nevada Smith
Tony Orlando
Jerry Paris
Nancy Poland
Portland Mason
Dolores Del Rio

Eddie Rochester
    Anderson
Sydne Rome*
Chicago
Seattle Slew
Jackie De Shannon
Sidney Greenstreet*
Sophia Loren
David Soul
Fay Spain
Dusty Springfield
Sylvia Sydney
Tennessee Ernie Ford
Tennessee Williams
Troy Donahue
Kenneth Turan
Victoria Principal
Virginia Graham
Dinah Washington
George Washington
Isaac Washington
Martha Washington
India Wilkes
Michael York

Glittering Prizes

How does one explain George Hamilton? Let's see . . . George is the kind of man who tans while everyone around him burns. A man who once had his Rolls Royce repainted to match the color of his date's eyes. A first date at that! George Hamilton is a man with style. A man who lives as if Hollywood were still Hollywood. Sitting poolside with George, trying not to perspire, watching his tan get darker right before my eyes, I ask him whether he can name some people you find in a jewelry store, like Neil Diamond, or Minnie Pearl. He and the rest of the star-studded group came up with some gems . . . What about you?

Give yourself 4 points for each answer.

Ray Reese

GEORGE HAMILTON	Crystal Gayle
DR. JOYCE BROTHERS	Ruby Keeler
MARILU HENNER	Rock Hudson
GEORGE HAMILTON	Ring Lardner
BETTY WHITE	Neil Diamond
TONY ORLANDO	Pearl Bailey
BEN VEREEN	Ruby Dee
FRANCESCO	

Patrick Terrail

SCAVULLO	Minnie Pearl
PETER MARSHALL	Billy Crystal
BOBBY SHORT	Jack Ruby
JIMMY BRESLIN	I. F. Stone
MAUREEN McCORMICK	Sly and the Family Stone
REX REED	Sterling Moss
GEORGE HAMILTON	Sterling Hayden
BRETT SOMERS	Jan Sterling
DAVID BRENNER	Jules Verne
MARY BETH McDONOUGH	The Rolling Stones
GEORGE HAMILTON	Long John Silver
JED ALLEN	Ron Glass
MILTON BERLE	Sapphire
GENE RAYBURN	Selma Diamond
JAMES KOMACK	China Lee
PATRICK TERRAIL	Ivory Joe Hunter
GEORGE HAMILTON	Johnny Cash

Prince Charles's Royal Names

Talked to Prince Charles this morning. I said, "Hi, Prince!" as his motorcade swept by. That's not true. Actually, His Royal Highness, the one future king of Great Britain and the shrinking dominions beyond the sea is quite an affable young man with considerable style and wit, which might have stood him in good stead in the theatre district of London's West End had he not been "to the purple born."

Being the Prince of Wales and heir presumptive to the throne is a pretty good job, you know! I mean, you don't have to worry about being canceled every thirteen weeks, or about not making a lucrative paperback sale. You do have to smile a lot, but nobody ever turns off your telephone if you were busy launching a battleship or something and forgot to pay the bill. If you're the Prince of Wales, someone else does your laundry! You can get a table at Sardi's! Norman Mailer might consent to talk to you (but this is doubtful . . .). Truman Capote would invite you to dinner though, you can count on it!

I'm sitting in the Regency Hotel on Nottingham Place reading a note from H.R.H., or rather from his embassy. It's on Buckingham Palace stationery, the good stuff, from Smithson over on Bond Street. It's pretty classy when Mum's picture is on the stamp and your personal secretary holds the rank of squadron leader.

Now, what does one say if one is given the opportunity to approach the Prince of Wales? On such an occasion one cannot avoid the realization that this gracious young man is the living personification of the Empire; the blood of a hundred kings and queens from eighth-grade history pulses, e'en at this very moment, through those charming veins. This man is the rightful successor to George III, defender of the faith. Descendant of Victoria and Albert. Son of Philip, Duke of Edinburge. The royal symbol of everything for which those gallant men upon the playing fields of Eton once reached out and shook the world. This man embodies the spirit of the Khyber Pass, Mountbatten and the Punjab, Churchill, Lord Nelson, Lawrence, and the Burma Road. This is Charles, the Earl of Chester, Duke of Cornwall and Rothsay, Earl of Carrick, Baron Renfrew, Lord of the Isles and Great Steward of Scotland. This is the Prince of Wales! This man knows the Queen of England personally!

What to say? The imagination reels at the possibilities. Should one inform the Prince of Wales that one has met the royal personage once before, at a private dinner party in Los Angeles? Would it be presumptuous to recall that one of my ancestors once served his by stealing enemy horses at Bosworth Field, or that another ancestor, in the defense of Wales, spilled the blood of his distant kin from Offa's Dyke to Swansea? Does one smile and ask him how it's going?

His Highness is regally outfitted in a dark pinstripe from Saville Row. The shirt is from Turnbull and Asser of Jermyn Street—one hundred thirty bucks a throw. He may be the future king of England, but at the moment, silence reigns. Any query or other utterance ventured must be properly phrased and presented. I mean, it is one thing to approach Bette Midler backstage at the London

Palladium, but this is quite another matter. This calls for a modicum of decorum, some elementary elocutionary eloquence, some sense of protocol. "May it please His Majesty, we are looking for famous people with royal titles in their names."

H.R.H. PRINCE CHARLES	Duke Ellington, Count Basie, Claude Dauphin
PETER USTINOV	King Kong
REGINE	Martin Luther King
TWIGGY	Patty Duke Astin
BRUCE FORSYTH	B. B. King
SIR FREDDIE LAKER	Ellery Queen
MICKEY ROONEY	Alan King
ELIZABETH ASHLEY	Alexander King
BETTY WHITE	King Vidor
TONY ORLANDO	Nat King Cole
BEN VEREEN	Morgana King
JIMMY BRESLIN	Duke Mantee
JOEL GREY	Hal Prince
PAT HARRINGTON	Freddie Prinze
MILTON BERLE	Duke Snyder
MORT SAHL	Earl "Fatha" Hines
DICK MARTIN	Earl Holliman
BETTY WHITE	Jack Lord
MARILU HENNER	Diana Prince
JAMES KOMACK	Arnie Sultan
DAVID BRENNER	Earl Warren
BOBBY SHORT	James Earl Jones
BOBBY VINTON	Mickey King
DR. JOYCE BROTHERS	Coretta King

Mickey Rooney

NADIA COMANECI   Billie Jean King
TONY DANZA   Carole King
BOB HOPE   Angier Biddle Duke
FRANCESCO
SCAVULLO   Shirley Knight
GEORGE BURNS   Gladys Knight and the
    Pips

Names You Can Find in a Garden

I was supposed to be at Lucie Arnaz's house 20 minutes ago, I left my tape recorder at Martoni's, where I had lunch (or else in the men's room of the Chevron station), and the studio page just interrupted Twiggy to inform me that my car is parked in Johnny Carson's spot. Other than that, things are fine!

Later, going through my notes, I discover that the hastily scribbled answers to most of the questions I managed to ask today are totally undecipherable. I am just able to discern that the category is famous names you can find in a garden, like Pete Rose, Ava Gardner, or Twiggy. Our celebrity team, whose members were Twiggy, Robert Shields, Lucie Arnaz, Lorene Yarnell, Pat Harrington, and Bruce Forsyth, came up with an impressive total of 60 acceptable answers. You may find more.

Take 1 point for each answer and a special 5-point bonus if, like our celebrities, you can think up a surprise or two!

BRUCE FORSYTH	Twiggy
TWIGGY	The Beatles
ROBERT SHIELDS	Adam West and Eve Arden*

LUCIE ARNAZ	Vincent Gardenia
LORENE YARNELL	George Bush
PAT HARRINGTON	Claire Bloom
BRUCE FORSYTH	Bea Lillie*
TWIGGY	Chauncey Gardner
ROBERT SHIELDS	Buddy Holly*
LUCIE ARNAZ	Leif Garrett
LORENE YARNELL	Orson Bean
PAT HARRINGTON	Wilt Chamberlain*
BRUCE FORSYTH	Earth, Wind and Fire*
TWIGGY	The Nitty Gritty Dirt Band*
ROBERT SHIELDS	Bugs Bunny
LUCIE ARNAZ	Moss Hart
LORENE YARNELL	Lorne Greene
PAT HARRINGTON	Don Ho*
BRUCE FORSYTH	Bud Abbott
TWIGGY	Pete Rose
ROBERT SHIELDS	Petunia Pig
LUCIE ARNAZ	Gunter Grass*
LORENE YARNELL	Roger Mudd*
PAT HARRINGTON	Butterfly McQueen*
BRUCE FORSYTH	Arthur Ashe
TWIGGY	Elihu Root
ROBERT SHIELDS	Basil Rathbone
LUCIE ARNAZ	The Great Waldo Pepper
LORENE YARNELL	Jiminy Cricket
PAT HARRINGTON	Ken Berry
BRUCE FORSYTH	Holly Woodlawn
TWIGGY	Chuck Berry
ROBERT SHIELDS	Ivy Baker Priest
LUCIE ARNAZ	Abe Burrows*
LORENE YARNELL	Daisy Mae
PAT HARRINGTON	Karen De Crow*
BRUCE FORSYTH	Claude Rains*
TWIGGY	Sluggo*
ROBERT SHIELDS	Beetle Bailey**

LUCIE ARNAZ	Wayland Flowers
LORENE YARNELL	Huckleberry Hound
PAT HARRINGTON	Jack Webb and Spider Sabitch*
BRUCE FORSYTH	Olive Oyl
TWIGGY	Rosemary Clooney
ROBERT SHIELDS	Ethel Waters
LUCIE ARNAZ	Muddy Waters**
LORENE YARNELL	Swee'pea
PAT HARRINGTON	Art Fern
BRUCE FORSYTH	Cliff Potts*
TWIGGY	Gene Weed*
ROBERT SHIELDS	Gypsy Rose Lee
LUCIE ARNAZ	Lily Tomlin
LORENE YARNELL	Alfalfa
PAT HARRINGTON	Clay Shaw
BRUCE FORSYTH	Richard Sickle
TWIGGY	Iris Carrington
ROBERT SHIELDS	The Carnation Company
LUCIE ARNAZ	Tokyo Rose
LORENE YARNELL	Sterling Moss
PAT HARRINGTON	Sam Spade*

People with Names You Could Find in a Workshop

Tony Orlando

In Las Vegas one night at about three o'clock in the morning I was wandering the streets with Tony Orlando; I asked him if he could name some people whose names you could find in a workshop, such as Natalie Wood, or Mike Hammer.

Can you think of 15 answers, as Tony did? Take 5 points per answer and an extra 15 points if you manage to think of 15 answers. Tony's responses are on the next page.

1. _____

2. _____

3. _____

4. _____

5. _____

6. _____

7. _____

8. _____

9. _____

10. _____

11. _____

12. _____

13. _____

14. _____

15. _____

1. Karen Carpenter 2. Johnny
Bench 3. Natalie Wood 4. Jim
Fixx 5. The Vice Squad
6. Richard Carpenter 7. Mike
Hammer 8. Peter O'Toole
9. Brad Balfour 10. Alex Cord
11. James Bond 12. Janice Rule
13. Jim Beam 14. Studs Lonigan
15. Studs Terkel

Famous Names that Fly

*

This is a question I posed to almost all of our celebrities. It is one of the most challenging, with literally hundreds of answers that will hover at the edge of consciousness and then pop into your mind at the most inopportune moments. So don't be surprised if you wake up suddenly mumbling Walter Pidgeon's name.

I have chosen a few answers from each of our celebrities, including some that are technically unacceptable but are just too good to pass up. The celebrities were assisted in this instance by sorority and fraternity representatives from the University of Missouri, Ohio State, and the University of Michigan at Ann Arbor. Each and every one came up with phenomenal answers.

Ben Vereen

Score 1 point for each of your answers and give yourself a 5-point bonus if you guess any of the starred items, which are particularly ingenious and come from the likes of Ben Vereen, Nadia Comaneci, and Madeline Kahn. Give yourself 10 points if you guess the incredible double-starred answer given by Steve Allen—Steve came up with a man whose first and last names both fly!

BEN VEREEN	Chicken George
FRANCESCO SCAVULLO	The Red Baron*
CALVIN KLEIN	Cardinal Cushing*
JIMMY BRESLIN	Goose Tatum
NADIA COMENECI	Superman*
DAVID NIVEN	Donald Duck
PRISCILLA PRESLEY	Robin Williams
ELIZABETH TAYLOR	Christopher Robin
LUCIE ARNAZ	Peter Pan*
DAVID BRENNER	Charlie's Angels*
MADELINE KAHN	Butterfly McQueen
ELIZABETH ASHLEY	Karen De Crow
TONI TENNILLE	Barbara Seagull
DEAN JONES	Walter Pidgeon
BIANCA JAGGER	Wings*
BOBBY SHORT	Leonard Feather*
BOB HOPE	Lady Bird Johnson
RICHARD HATCH	The Maltese Falcon
PAT HARRINGTON	Bugs Moran*
DICK MARTIN	The Spirit of St. Louis*
VERNON JORDAN	Lucky Lindy*
CRAIG CLAIBORNE	Amelia Earhart
ANDREW YOUNG	Douglas "Wrong Way" Corrigan
TOM BRADLEY	Wiley Post
BETTY WHITE	Jeanne Crain
MILTON BERLE	Bob Crane
PETER USTINOV	Kenneth Peacock Tynan*
ROBERT SHIELDS	Molly Bee*
SEN. JOHN WARNER	Florence Nightingale
STEVE ALLEN	Egel Crogh
SEN. TED KENNEDY	John Jay
LORENE YARNELL	Falcon Eddy*
MARILYN CHAMBERS	Woody Woodpecker

Steve Allen

James Komack

Tony Danza

Mickey Rooney

SEASON HUBLEY	Toby Wing
ZANDRA RHODES	Robin Cook
SEN. CHARLES PERCY	Gil Scott Heron
ALEXIS SMITH	Senator Robert Byrd
KURT RUSSELL	Roman Gabriel*
SIR FREDDIE LAKER	Freddie Laker*
NICHELLE NICHOLS	The Starship Enterprise*
TONY DANZA	Sky King
GLORIA VANDERBILT	Woodstock
SUSAN ANTON	Rick "Goose" Gossage
PIERRE TRUDEAU	Led Zeppelin*
ED ASNER	Pontius Pilate
DR. JOYCE BROTHERS	The Partridge Family*
ROLF HARRIS	Anthony Quayle
DICK VAN PATTEN	Jeanne Eagles
WYOMIA TYUS	The Byrds
LIBERACE	Big Bird
MARK GOODSON	Admiral Byrd
MORT SAHL	Charlie "Bird" Parker
SOPHIA LOREN	Christopher Wren
SHARI LEWIS	Conrad Birdie
TONY ORLANDO	Lynn Swan
PATRICK TERRAIL	Meadowlark Lemon
MORGAN FAIRCHILD	The Eagles
ANN JILLIAN	The Jefferson Airplane*
JUDITH KRANZ	Rooster Cogburn
VIDAL SASSOON	The Beatles
MICKEY ROONEY	Howard Hawks
REX REED	Rocket J. Squirrel*

Women Who Have Men's Names

I recently had the pleasure of spending some time with Toni Tennille. In a town and a business where people might be excused for being blasé, Toni is more than a breath of fresh air; she's a Santa Ana whirlwind. Toni and her executive producer, Mike Hill, made it possible for us to get to many of the celebrities who appear here.

One afternoon, I asked Toni and Mike if they could come up with some famous women who have men's names. They had a lot of fun and came up with quite a few, as you shall see. (Wonder if you can guess who the very last one was . . .) But first exercise your own gray cells on this one.

Take 3 points for each such lady you think of, 5 points for your answers that match Toni's and Mike's bonus answers(*), and 10 points for the double bonuses(**).

Billie Holiday
Billie Jean King
Bobbie Gentry
Bo Derek
Ronee Blakely

Michael Learned
Taylor Caldwell**
Georges Sand**
Frankie Fitzgerald**
Lee Grant**

Billie Burke*
Sydney Goldsmith
Sydne Rome
Morgan Brittany*
Bobbie Fiedler

The game ended with the following exchange between Toni and Mike:

MIKE   Can you think of any more?

TONI   Yeah, I've got a good one.

MIKE   Someone in show business?

TONI   Yeah, a superstar.

MIKE   I give up! Who is it?

TONI   Toni Tennille!

MIKE   Oh . . . You're not going to print this?

Hot and Cold

With the possible exception of Orson Welles, no one commands attention in a crowded room like Peter Ustinov. Peter is a great teddy bear of a man who laughs each time, as if it were something he had learned how to do.

Someone once asked Peter if he wouldn't have preferred to live in the sixteenth century. "The sixteenth century?" Peter bellowed. "Can you imagine what it would be like to have a toothache in the sixteenth century?"

That's the kind of mind you're up against here. I asked Mr. Ustinov to think of famous names that are hot and cold—Hank Snow or Sonny Bono, for example. Take 4 points for each answer.

Here is Mr. Ustinov's incredible list.

HOT: Gabriel *Heater*, *Sonny* Liston, Donna *Summer*, Rev. *Sun* Myung *Moon*, *Blaze* Starr, George *Burns*, *Sonny* Bono, Leonard *Frye*, Suzanne *Somers*, Northrop *Frye*, Peter *Boyle*.

COLD: David *Frost*, Paul *Winter*, Edgar *Winter*, *Cool* Hand Luke, Raymond *Burr*, Nathan *Hale*, Jonathan *Winters*, Phoebe *Snow*, Aaron *Burr*, Hank *Snow*, *Chill* Wills.

HOT	COLD
1. _____	1. _____
2. _____	2. _____
3. _____	3. _____
4. _____	4. _____
5. _____	5. _____
6. _____	6. _____
7. _____	7. _____
8. _____	8. _____
9. _____	9. _____
10. _____	10. _____
11. _____	11. _____

Famous Names That You Can Find in the Bathroom

Hollywood   We are sitting around Joyce Selznick's table in a dining room paneled with rustic boards, taken from an old barn in Maine. The chandelier is from a chateau in the south of France.

President of a highly successful talent conglomerate, author of *Blue Roses,* descended from both the Selznicks and the Warners, Joyce Selznick is Hollywood. Her cousin made *Gone With the Wind.* She herself is the woman who discovered Richard Dreyfuss, Faye Dunaway, and Candice Bergen, to name just a few, and, more important, she is a good friend and gives the best parties west of the Rockies.

Tonight is no exception. Shirley MacLaine is seated over near the fireplace. In the music room Brenda Vaccaro and Anna Moffo are holding forth. The cobblestone patio and the jacuzzi are out there somewhere, obscured by the likes of Charlene Tilton, Loretta Swit, Rock Hudson, Dr. Irene Kassorla and Jan McCormick, Joyce's partner. Suddenly the music stops, and the surprised assemblage hears Joyce announce that everyone is going to be in my new book!

Damn! Now I have to think of a question. I was on my way to the loo. "Hmmm . . . that's not a bad idea!" How about some FAMOUS NAMES YOU CAN FIND IN THE BATHROOM (like Ernest Tubb or Earl Butz).

Score 5 points for each answer you come up with. Are you going to let the celebrities beat you at this?

Here are some of the inventive answers shouted out over the heads of the celebrities at Ms. Selznick's party.

Timothy Bottoms	Fannie Flagg	Christopher Plummer
John Bubbles	Ron Glass	Georgie Tapps
Earl Butz	Edith Head	Ernest Tubb
Jerry Colonna	Elton John	Ethel Waters
Jane Curtin	Sybil Leek	W. C. Fields
Farrah Fawcett	Matt Dillon	

People with Diminutive Names

New York   **I**f you're in New York with only a few hours to spend, then Mabel Mercer, lunch at the Algonquin Hotel, and Bobby Short at the Café Carlyle are the three things that you shouldn't miss.

I phoned Bobby when I was in New York a few weeks ago, and he was in the south of France. That's one of the things that I like about him. Bobby Short lives life as if it were a Cole Porter lyric. He's been kissed by Margaux Hemingway and hugged by both the Bouvier girls. He knew Bea Lillie! The chances are that if you were to stop a sample of celebrities in the streets of St. Tropez and ask them who best exemplifies the word *style,* Bobby Short would win, hands down on the Steinway!

When we were finally able to track Bobby down at his tropical greenhouse apartment near Carnegie Hall, we leaned back in the tall, rattan chairs and asked Mr. Short whether he would be kind enough to try PEOPLE WITH DIMINUTIVE NAMES, like *Bobby Short* or *Little Richard.*

As you can see, nicknames also count. Give yourself 3 points for each answer and 5 points if you can match his tiny bonuses (*).

Li'l Abner*   Tawny Little   Minnie Mouse*
Little Boy Blue   Little Red Riding Hood Minnie Minosa*
Little Jimmy Dickens   Little Richard   Pee Wee Reese*
Little Orphan Annie   Three Little Pigs*   Bobby Short
Little Annie Fanny   Rich Little   Shorty Rodgers
Little Miss Muffet   The Little River Band   Tiny Tim* and
Little Beaver   The Micronauts   Tiny Tim*
Ten Little Indians*   Minnie Pearl*   Wee Willie Winkie*

Names You Might Hear on the Weather Report/Names You Can find on a Map

On an off-duty afternoon, in the middle of chatting about something else, I hit Mike Douglas and Lucie Arnaz with two unrelated categories, one after the other, just to see how fast they could change gears.

They did so well that I am including both questions here. Let's find out how quickly you can switch your mind from one ludicrous category to another.

First I asked them to try and imagine some FAMOUS NAMES YOU MIGHT HEAR ON THE WEATHER REPORT, like Claude Rains or Hank Snow. Score 3 points for each of your answers and 5 points for any of the starred items you guess.

Finally, I asked Mike and Lucie for some NAMES YOU FIND ON THE MAP, like Steve Canyon or Glenn Ford. Take a well-deserved 1 point for each answer and a special bonus of 35 points if you can match all of their 66 incredible answers.

Here are 28 names from the weather report.

Gale Storm *
Kool and the Gang
Nathan Hale
Sonny Bono

David Frost
Tempest Storm *
Hank Snow
Claude Rains

Wendy Barrie
Hale Boggs
Edgar Winter
Misty Rowe *

Curt Flood *
Jack Frost
Ford Rainey
Phoebe Snow
Grace Slick *
Chief Thundercloud *

Red Cloud
Snow White
Chill Wills
Chief Rain in the Face
Hale Irwin

Robert Frost
Crystal Gayle
Alan Hale
A. A. Fair
Sonny Tufts

Here are Mike and Lucie's names you can find on a map:

Sheree North
Packy East
Mr. and Mrs. North
Joe South
Joe Pass
Arthur Hill
Benny Hill
Fanny Hill
Graham Hill
Phil Hill
Edwin Knoll
Abbey Lane
Veronica Lake
Edwin Land
Mark Lane
Frankie Laine
Mary Tyler Moore
Roger Moore
Man Mountain Dean
Dale Evans
Eartha Kitt
Senator Edward Brookes
Arthur Lake

Brooke Shields
Carrie Nation
Country Joe and the Fish
Gertrude Berg
Brooke Bundy
Mel Brooks
Cliff Robertson
Mary Baker Eddy
Sally Field
Gracie Fields
W. C. Fields
Forrest Tucker
Glen Campbell
Glenn Ford
Lefty Grove
Edward Heath
Jean Marsh
Audrey Meadows
Jayne Meadows
Vera Miles
Miles Davis
Rand McNally
Freddie Fields

Hamlet
Danny Ocean
Paddy Chayefsky
Tongson Park
Louis Pasteur
Bernard Shurcliff
Joan Rivers
Dusty Rhodes
Talia Shire
Robert Towne
Dinah Shore
Rudy Vallee
Mae West
Jerry West
The Village People
James Woods
Jerry Quarry
Bert Parks
Della Street
Jerry Vale
Dr. Edward Land
Mary Kay Place

Famous People with a Color in Their Names

Las Vegas It is 11:36 and the Las Vegas strip is just now yawning and waking up. Blackjack dealers and Keno girls are knocking off for lunch, and a couple of thousand hookers are getting ready to go to work, pressing the wrinkles out of their Dior gowns and Halston pantsuits.

Inside the Riviera Hotel, in Tony Orlando's dressing room, the man himself greets me with a shout and a hug. He is dressed in a black robe and a stylish black gaucho hat, and I tell him he looks like Zorro. He laughs.

Before I go any further, I'd like to say what a valuable contribution Tony Orlando made to this book. Tony got us to David Brenner. Tony told half the headliners in Vegas about this strange book I was doing, so that when I phoned they were primed and ready. When Tony Orlando hugs you, you stay hugged.

Halfway through my interview with Tony, there is a knock on the door and Ben Vereen sticks his head inside.

Instant bedlam!

Ben is accompanied by his wife, son, secretary, and agent. Before anyone can even say hello, Tony grabs Ben and asks him if he can think of A FAMOUS PERSON WITH A COLOR IN HIS NAME.

Ben frowns. "Slappy White?" he asks, wondering

Ben Vereen

why we want to know. We tell him, and he's off. "Joel Grey . . . Vida Blue . . . Karen Black." "Lorne Greene," says Ben's wife, Nancy. "Redd Foxx!" This is from his son, Benjy. His secretary, Penelope Selwyn, comes up with "Scarlett O'Hara!"

"Wait a minute . . . give me a break!" Tony yells, wrestling with Ben. "Whitey Ford!"

"Boston Blackie!" Ben counters through Tony's headlock. "Tokyo Rose, Pink Floyd, The Lavender Hill Mob!!"

Score 1 point for each appropriate answer, 2 points for each bonus (*) answer.

Black Sabbath*	Coco Chanel	Pinky Tuscadero*
Boston Blackie*	James Coco	Red Barber
Justice Hugo Black	Andrew Gold	The Red Baron*
Karen Black	Harry Golden	Red Buttons
Shirley Temple Black	The Green Hornet*	Chief Red Cloud
The Blue Angels*	Adolph Green	Don "Red" Barry
Ben Blue	Gerald Green	Red Foley
Vida Blue	Graham Greene	Redd Foxx
Little Boy Blue*	Johnny Green	Red Grange
The Brown Bomber*	Lorne Greene	Red Nichols
Bobby Brown	The Jolly Green Giant*	Red Norvo
Buster Brown*	Mean Joe Green	Red Ryder*
Charlie Brown*	Peter Green	Little Red Riding
Georg Sanford Brown	Richard Greene	Hood*
Helen Gurley Brown	Dorian Grey*	Red Rover*
Jackson Browne	Joel Grey	Red Schoendienst
James Brown	Lady Jane Grey	Red Skelton
Jim Brown	Zane Grey	Rose La Rose*
Joe E. Brown	Ivory Joe Hunter*	Billy Rose
John Brown	Lavender Hill Mob	David Rose
Johnny Mack Brown	The Pink Panther*	Gypsy Rose Lee
Les Brown	Pink Floyd*	Rose Kennedy
Ray Brown	Pinky Lee	Pete Rose

Tokyo Rose
Rosey Grier
Rosie O'Grady
Harold Scarlet
Scarlett O'Hara
Will Scarlet
Long John Silver*

Ultra Violet*
Barry White
Betty White
E. B. White
Jesse White
Justice Byron White
Patrick White

Perry White*
Slappy White
Stanford White
Wilfred Hyde-White
Theodore White
Whitey Ford

...AND STILL
MORE THINGS

What Kind of Car Would They Be?

Among the best times that I had doing these interviews was when I asked Elizabeth Ashley and Art Buchwald to try and imagine some of their fellow celebrities as cars. I have listed those responses and the celebrities they were describing along with appropriate space for your own answers so that you can match your wits against theirs.

First however, I would be remiss if I didn't practice what I preach and tell you that I see Art Buchwald as a Ford two-door, the standard model, but with a 1500 horsepower, finely-tuned Ferrari Dino hidden under the hood just waiting for some unsuspecting fool to pull up beside him and rev the engine.

Ms. Ashley is, of course, a classic 1938 LaGonda Drophead Coupe with her top down in the rain.

Elizabeth Ashley

Here are the celebrities which we asked Art Buchwald and Elizabeth Ashley to describe as a kind of car.

Try it yourself before you turn the page and attempt to figure out what Art and Elizabeth said.

Truman Capote would be _____

Johnny Carson would be _____

Burt Reynolds would be _____

Ronald Reagan would be _____

Margaret Thatcher would be _____

Richard Nixon would be _____

Bette Midler would be _____

Jimmy Carter would be _____

Remember, here are the people that Art and Elizabeth
were talking about.

Truman Capote   Burt Reynolds
Jimmy Carter   Richard Nixon
Johnny Carson   Ronald Reagan
Bette Midler   Margaret Thatcher

See if you tell Art's quotes from Elizabeth's and who
they were describing. Take 5 points for each blank
you fill correctly and a 10 point bonus if the car that
came to your mind previously matches our celebrities.

THEY SAID IT   ABOUT

_____ said   "_____ is an
                       Edsel!"

_____ said   "_____ is a
                       Pinto, sooner or later the
                       son of a bitch is going to
                       kill you!

_____ said   "_____ would
                       have to be a perfectly
                       polished, 300 SL
                       Mercedes!"

THEY SAID IT	ABOUT
_____ said	"_____ would be a Sherman Tank!"
_____ said	"_____ has got to be a Corvair!"
_____ said	"_____ would be a Moped!"
_____ said	"_____ is a second-hand classic!"
_____ said	"_____ Just your basic Pinto!"
_____ said	"_____ would be something with lots of style; lots of power under the hood and a cute little rear end!"

No one can ever accuse Art Buchwald or Elizabeth Ashley of being afraid to express an opinion.

THEY SAID IT	ABOUT
Art Buchwald said	"Ronald Reagan is an Edsel!"
Elizabeth Ashley said	"Ronald Reagan is a Pinto, sooner or later the son of a bitch is going to kill you!"
Elizabeth Ashley said	"Johnny Carson would have to be a perfectly polished, 300 SL Mercedes!"

THEY SAID IT	ABOUT
Art Buchwald said	"Margaret Thatcher would be a Sherman Tank!"
Elizabeth Ashley said	"Richard Nixon has got to be a Corvair!"
Art Buchwald said	"Truman Capote would be a Moped!"
Elizabeth Ashley said	"Bette Midler is a second-hand classic!"
Art Buchwald said	"Jimmy Carter? Just your basic Pinto!"
Elizabeth Ashley said	"Burt Reynolds would be something with lots of style, lots of power under the hood and a cute little rear end!"

If X Were a Piece of Furniture . . .

Catalina Island
California

Tony Orlando

Ben Vereen

After awhile, a project such as this one begins to take on a life of its own. One day I innocently asked Ben Vereen and Tony Orlando for immediate, one-word reactions to other celebrities' names. This soon turned into "What would Richard Nixon be if he were a piece of furniture . . ." Elizabeth Ashley decided she would personally rather tell me what kind of food she imagined Burt Reynolds to be. In the south of France, the question for Art Buchwald became "If Truman Capote were a car . . ."

Let's start with the reactions of 10 of our celebrities when they were asked what kind of furniture a particular world-famous personality would be—if he were a piece of furniture . . . The 10 celebrities were:

Jed Allen   Tony Orlando
Elizabeth Ashley   Mort Sahl
Ed Asner   Ben Vereen
Dr. Joyce Brothers   Dick Van Patten
Marilyn Chambers   Betty White

All of these celebrity statements describe the same man. If you can identify him, it's worth 100 points. You will find the answer at the bottom of the next page.

121

Ben Vereen said	I don't know, but he'd be the first thing that caught your eye when you entered the room.
Ed Asner said	A great, antique, English roll-top desk that's always locked.
Marilyn Chambers said	A throne.
Joyce Brothers said	One of those wonderful big overstuffed chairs that everybody races to get to first. Real leather. I've always thought that it would be nice to cuddle up in his lap.
Dick Van Patton said	The kind of furniture that they don't make anymore!
Jed Allen said	An enormous Victorian dining-room table. Handmade!
Mort Sahl said	Furniture that's out of work! Something that's in a thrift shop window somewhere because it makes all this Danish Modern crap look like crap.
Tony Orlando said	A concert grand piano! The kind of thing you build the room around. Exactly what I'd like to be if I were a piece of furniture.
Betty White said	A big brown leather bean bag.
Elizabeth Ashley said	Something that you get up in the middle of the night to polish. A great big armoire, massive, dark, and secretive . . . with an enormous mirror on the doors that looks right through you. Henry VIII's armoire. Definitely!

Answer: Orson Welles

Sticks and Stones

Now that you're in a furniture mood, let's try to imagine what kind of furniture a whole collection of famous personalities might be. This time I have listed in one group the celebrities who gave us the answers and in another group the famous personalities they are describing. You will notice that there are four quotes from Betty White. They were all just too good to pass up.

Give yourself 5 points if you can match the personality with the description, and 5 more if you can guess who said it—plus a 10-point bonus if you get everything right. Answers are at the bottom of page 124.

Ed Asner

Betty White

Betty White	Johnny Carson
Elizabeth Ashley	Burt Reynolds
Dr. Joyce Brothers	Jimmy Carter
Betty White	Ed McMahon
Marilyn Chambers	Richard Nixon
Betty White	Lauren Hutton
Ed Asner	Cher
and Betty White were	and Betty White
describing	

THEY SAID IT	ABOUT

1. _____

_____ is a reupholstered sofa. It looks great but you know that if you ever decide to go over there and sit down, (s)he's gonna shove a spring up your behind!

2. _____

_____ would be one of those very expensive glass and chrome coffee tables. Always polished, filled with lots of wonderfully interesting things arranged just perfectly, and God help you if you reach out to touch one of them!

3. _____

_____ is a loveseat. It's a great idea, but it doesn't work!

4. _____

_____ is a Queen Anne crewel back chair. Very elegant. The kind that everybody wants to jump on, but no one ever does.

5. _____

_____ has got to be a motel bed!

6. _____

_____ is just "everyday furniture," Sears and Roebuck with a paint job!

7. _____

_____ I think, would be a hassock. Always there, right where you left it. Comfortable. Something that you look forward to getting home to.

8. _____

_____ is a very strange chest of drawers. Just drawers, no chest!

If Mickey Rooney Were a Toy, What Kind of Toy Would He Be?

*The Mickey Rooney
Tavas Hotel
Downingtown,
Pennsylvania*

What can I tell you about Mickey Rooney? Once when for some strange reason I was involved in an interminably boring meeting concerning the construction of a prospective "Hollywood" museum—a permanent place to display Judy's Red Shoes and the Duke's Eyepatch—I suggested that they forget the whole thing and put up a statue of Mickey Rooney! Mickey and Wallace Beery at the corner of Hollywood and Vine! Tourists could rub his nose for luck and carve the name of their home town along his base.

At one time, an entire generation of Americans, including me, ran away to join the circus or entered some form of the entertainment arts because of Mickey. Even today, the best training that any young performer could ever hope for would be to spend a few minutes in the same room with him. Better yet, go over to the theatre and watch him work, and then go back and watch him work again. Mickey may be the last, best example of what American show business started out to be: three a day on the Orpheum circuit, pathos and pratfalls, gold watches and popcorn hawked during the intermission. In my purely personal opinion, an old 8 × 10 MGM glossy of Mickey and Judy Garland still is more entertaining than anything Scorsese or Cimino can put on the screen for 30 or 40 million dollars.

Mickey Rooney

125

If you're in New York and you're tired of going over to Liza's for pasta and you don't know anyone who can fix you up with Lauren Hutton, go watch Mickey; it's the next best thing.

All right, with Mr. Rooney's help let's try another one of those interpretive questions I threw at our celebrities without warning. Remember, the answers you see here are their spontaneous reactions, right off the tops of their infamous heads. This time I asked Mickey and the rest of the gang: "If _____were a toy, what toy would he or she be?" The "toys" described by our celebrities were: Helen Gurley Brown, Art Buchwald, Mickey Rooney, Johnny Carson, Ronald Reagan, John Travolta, Robert Blake, Jimmy Carter, Doc Severinson, Ed McMahon, Cher, and Paul Williams. Here's a clue: One of these famous people is describing him- or herself.

Score 10 points for a successful match of celebrity to "toy" and a 10-point bonus if you get them all. Answers at the bottom of page 127.

1 . BETTY WHITE _____ has to be a really great-looking remote-control car with dead batteries.

2 . ED ASNER _____ would be a Tonka truck or a pet rock, something indestructable.

3 . KURT RUSSELL If _____ were a toy she'd be a jump rope!

4 . MARILU HENNER

_____? Ha! A Let's-play-doctor kit.

5 . LAURIE WALTERS _____ would be something cuddly, with one of those strings coming out of his back that you pull and he says exactly what you want to hear!

6 . ELIZABETH ASHLEY If _____ were a toy? I don't know, but I wouldn't let my kid play with him!

7. BEN VEREEN   _____ would be a finger-painting set, or maybe a Slinky!

8. DR. JOYCE BROTHERS   If _____ were a toy he'd have to be a big lovable overstuffed panda.

9. JIMMY BRESLIN   If she were a toy, _____ would be some kind of doll. I never got to play with them when I was growing up, but she'd be some really classy Dresden doll, made in New Jersey, tough and smart!

10. MARILYN CHAMBERS   _____ would be a Ken Doll and if I were Barbie I wouldn't leave him home alone with Betsy-Wetsy!

11. MICKEY ROONEY   If _____ were a toy, he'd be an erector set take it down, put it up, it still works!

12. HELEN GURLEY BROWN   _____ has to be a Gund teddy bear.

1. Jimmy Carter 2. Robert Blake 3. Cher 4. John Travolta 5. Paul Williams 6. Ronald Reagan 7. Doc Severinson 8. Ed McMahon 9. Helen Gurley Brown 10. Johnny Carson 11. Mickey Rooney 12. Art Buchwald

Really Built

Mort Sahl

We asked Lucie Arnaz, Peter Ustinov, Mort Sahl, Marilyn Chambers, Mary Beth McDonough, Charlene Tilton, Tony Orlando, Marilu Henner, and Ben Vereen to describe some of their peers as buildings: If X WERE A BUILDING HE/SHE WOULD BE _____. See how well you do at deciding what kind of building our celebrities thought the people listed below would be.

Robert Redford
Goldie Hawn
Orson Welles
Faye Dunaway
G. Gordon Liddy

Richard Hatch
Bette Midler
Johnny Carson
Marlon Brando

Give yourself 10 points for each correct identification and a 10-point bonus for sweeping the category. Answers at the bottom of page 129.

1. LUCIE ARNAZ _____? With any luck he'd be my house!

2. MARILU HENNER If _____ were a building, he'd be the Louvre!

3. PETER USTINOV If _____ were a building, she'd be condemned.

128

4. BEN VEREEN	If _____ were a building, he'd be in Beverly Hills.
5. MARILYN CHAMBERS	If _____ were a building, she'd be a terrific whorehouse!
6. TONY ORLANDO	If _____ were a building, she'd be a Frank Lloyd Wright: classic, one of a kind.
7. CHARLENE TILTON	If _____ were a building? A really great-looking library.
8. MORT SAHL	If _____ were a building? No problem! The house at Amityville.
9. MARY BETH McDONOUGH	If _____ were a building, he'd sell himself to the highest bidder.

Ben Vereen

1. Richard Hatch 2. Orson Welles 3. Goldie Hawn 4. Johnny Carson 5. Bette Midler 6. Faye Dunaway 7. Robert Redford 8. G. Gordon Liddy 9. Marlon Brando

Celebrity Stew

Baja Peninsula
Mexico

The Mexican sun is shining down on the Sea of Cortez and there's not a telephone or a William Morris agent in sight. The only celebrity down here is Manuel: he knows where the trout are jumping and where to find the hot peppers and the cold Dos Equis beer.

Last night I met two young women in Santa Rosalia who are traveling through the Baja in a battered old Volkswagen camper on their way to South America, and then on to Africa, and then on to somewhere else. Here on the deserted beach of Concepcion Bay, multicolored birds are singing and doing something strange to themselves that they seem to like. Mexico has a marvelous way of letting you see things in the proper perspective. Today, tomorrow, or perhaps the day after, I am going to climb back on my motorcycle and ride on down to Cabo San Lucas to buy a newspaper. Later, after a little sun and some fresh fish, I might even read it. I am supposed to be in New York to meet Liza on the twentieth. Today is the fifteenth, I think. Close enough, relax!

I am offering you here some wonderful answers that give you a glimpse into the overactive minds of six highly diverse celebrities when their thoughts are ranging free. I asked Helen Gurley Brown, Art Buchwald, Betty White, Marilyn Chambers, Peter

Art Buchwald

Ustinov, and Elizabeth Ashley to imagine what a number of their contemporaries—and peers—might be if they were . . . anything. I let the celebrities interpret the question as they saw fit. See if you can discover whom the celebrities were describing.

Score 5 points for each correct pairing. Answers at the bottom of the page 133. Hint: One celebrity is described twice.

They were talking about:

Walter Cronkite	Walter Mondale
Lauren Bacall	Richard Nixon
Johnny Carson	Helen Gurley Brown
Bette Midler	Francesco Scavullo
Norman Mailer	Sammy Davis Jr.
Burt Reynolds	Ben Bradlee
Billy Carter	Jacqueline Onassis

1 . PETER USTINOV   If _____ were a food, he'd be inedible.

2 . ART BUCHWALD   _____ is a refrigerator.

3 . HELEN GURLEY BROWN   _____ would be a miniature Ferrari, the kind they sell at F.A.O. Schwartz. Beauty, drive, power, and precision wrapped up in one superior Italian product!

4 . ELIZABETH ASHLEY   _____? I don't know but I want seconds!

5 . BETTY WHITE   If he were a piece of furniture, _____ would be a leather Barcalounger.

6 . PETER USTINOV   If _____ were a place, she'd be Switzerland. Tiny and probably a little shy, but with enormous influence. A Swiss numbered account, hiding more than she's telling.

7 . ART BUCHWALD   _____ would have to be a doormat.

8. MARILYN CHAMBERS	If he were a toy, I see _____ as one of those paddle-ball things, which are so great because it's sort of like playing with yourself!
9. ART BUCHWALD	_____ would be a washbasin.
10. ART BUCHWALD	_____ would be a coatrack.
11. PETER USTINOV	_____ is the perfect pillow.
12. ART BUCHWALD	_____ is definitely a headrest.
13. ART BUCHWALD	If _____ were a kind of food, (s)he would be saltwater taffy.
14. PETER USTINOV	If she were food, _____ would be marshmallow!
15. MARILYN CHAMBERS	That's easy! If _____ were something to eat he'd be a Tootsie Roll—the big one.

In the course of all this questioning, the two names that brought forth the most immediate and positive responses were Orson Welles and Lauren Hutton. I would venture an uneducated guess that it has something to do with style. Burt Reynolds and Lauren Bacall also received raves whenever their names were mentioned. Not one of our celebrities had a negative image of them. I'm not sure what all this means, except that it might not be a bad idea to name your daughter Lauren.

On the other hand, the names of Jimmy Carter and Ronald Reagan were almost always received with a shrug or a full frontal attack. Bette Midler was either passionately loved or passionately hated. So was Ted Kennedy.

Richard Nixon and Suzanne Somers received just about the worst press from their peers. For example, when I asked, "Whom would you like not to read about anymore?" 53 celebrities named Nixon or Somers. Some other favorite answers to that question were: Robin Williams (14), Bo Derek (17), John Derek (almost unanimous), and Henry Kissinger (23). Honorable mention would go to Farrah Fawcett, Hamilton Jordan, and Cher.

Cher placed tops in the letch department with the gentlemen we interviewed. With the ladies, Burt Reynolds gets an "A" for lust. Not so different from the answers you might receive if you interviewed the freshman class at Ritenour High School.

1. Norman Mailer 2. Jacqueline Kennedy 3. Francesco Scavullo 4. Burt Reynolds 5. Walter Cronkite 6. Helen Gurley Brown 7. Billy Carter 8. Johnny Carson 9. Richard Nixon 10. Walter Mondale 11. Lauren Bacall 12. Lauren Bacall 13. Ben Bradlee 14. Bette Midler 15. Sammy Davis, Jr.

Cher

Las Vegas **W**hen I asked the male celebrities we spoke to WHOM THEY WOULD MOST LIKE TO MEET IF THEY COULD HAVE JUST ONE LAST FLING, we expected to hear Catherine Deneuve or Bo Derek, or Farrah Fawcett or Cheryl Ladd. The name we heard most often, however, was Cher's. It is also interesting to note that the mention of Cher's name very often caused our celebrities, both men and women, to blurt out answers and then ask that they be deleted from the tape, or at least not attributed to them.

Cher has a strange effect on people.

I presented several of our celebrities with these questions about Cher and asked them to fill in the blanks completely spontaneously—off the top of their heads. You are invited to do the same. When you are finished, see page 135 and match your wits with our celebrities', while at the same time attempting to figure out who said what about Cher.

Score 10 points for each correct identification of a celebrity's answer and a 5-point bonus if you had the same answer. There will be a final 10-point bonus and a lie detector test for anyone who matches all six answers.

1. If Cher were a building she'd be a _____.

2. If Cher were a toy she'd be _____.

3. If Cher were a car she'd be _____.

4. If Cher were a place she'd be _____.

5. If Cher were a piece of clothing she'd be _____.

6. If Cher were food she'd be _____.

The people who were willing to share their thoughts on Cher were Marilyn Chambers, Ed Asner, Elizabeth Ashley, Betty White, Joyce Selznick, and Richard Hatch. Try to pair each response with the right person. The answers are at the bottom of the page.

1. _____ If Cher were a building she'd be a motel.

2. _____ If Cher were a toy? A doll in leather with a whip. She'd glow in the dark!

3. _____ If Cher were a car she'd be on a used car lot. A Nash Rambler with those seats that become a bed and with a lot of good miles left on her!

4. _____ If Cher were a place? Times Square.

5. _____ Clothing? A garter belt and net hose. Spike heels and a feather boa!

6. _____ If Cher were a food she'd be junk food. It's great, but you know it's gonna keep you up all night.

1. Ed Asner 2. Marilyn Chambers 3. Richard Hatch 4. Joyce Selznick 5. Elizabeth Ashley 6. Betty White.

PERSONAL
INSIGHTS

Moroccan Leather

While having lunch one day in the Viennese Palm Court of the Plaza Hotel in New York, I noticed Rex Reed being escorted to a table at the far side of the room. With no preliminaries, I took my pen and scribbled this next test onto my napkin, called the waiter, and had it sent to Rex's table.

A couple of minutes later, the waiter was back and Rex was smiling. He had filled in all of the blanks I had drawn onto the napkin. Try it. Just put down the first thing that comes to mind for each word.

Give yourself 3 points for each answer. Take a 1-point bonus for each answer that matches one of Rex's.

Polish _____   French _____   Cuban _____

German _____   Irish _____   Japanese _____

Chinese _____   Swiss _____   American _____

Greek _____   Danish _____   Turkish _____

Dutch _____   Brazil _____   Belgian _____

English _____   Panama _____   Swedish _____

Russian _____   Scotch _____   Spanish _____

Here are Rex Reed's answers, which I saw when I unfolded the napkin (with the Plaza waiter watching and, I'm sure, wondering who was going to pay for the once beautiful linen napkin).

Polish	jokes	French	kiss	Cuban	refugees
German	measles	Irish	linen	Japanese	gardener
Chinese	checkers	Swiss	bank accounts	American	graffiti
Greek	Melina Mercouri	Danish	pastry	Turkish	prisons
Dutch	uncle	Brazil	nuts	Belgian	Hercule Poirot
English	muffins	Panama	Hattie	Swedish	meatballs
Russian	roulette	Scotch	rocks	Spanish	fly

REX REED'S BONUS

I almost missed it, but when I turned the napkin over I saw that Mr. Reed had added a little something of his own! Try it for 20 extra bonus points.

French _____	French _____	French _____
French _____	French _____	French _____
French _____	French _____	French _____
French _____	French _____	French _____
French _____	French _____	French _____
French _____	French _____	French _____

Here is Rex's fabulous French soliloquy!

French	postcards	French	fries	French	poodle
French	toast	French	leave	French	mistress
French	quarter	French	bread	French	Revolution
French	subtitles	French	horn	French	cuffs
French	Resistance	French	doors	French	dressing
French	Guiana	French	heels	French	Connection

140

While reviewing my tapes late one night, I discovered that Gore Vidal's voice played at the wrong speed sounds exactly the way Truman Capote sounds all the time. I also discovered that when Richard Hatch took this same test, he duplicated only one of Rex Reed's answers.

Polish _____	French _____	Cuban _____
German _____	Irish _____	Japanese _____
Chinese _____	Swiss _____	American _____
Greek _____	Danish _____	Turkish _____
Dutch _____	Brazil _____	Belgian _____
English _____	Panama _____	Swedish _____
Russian _____	Scotch _____	Spanish _____

Here are Richard Hatch's responses.

Polish	sausage	Irish	coffee	Japanese	beetle
German	shepherd	Swiss	cheese	American	pie
Chinese	fortune cookies	Danish	modern	Turkish	delight
Greek	tragedy	Brazil	Sergio Mendes & "66-67-?"	Belgian	waffles
Dutch	treat	Panama	Canal	Swedish	blondes
English	toffee	Scotch	tape	Spanish	fly*
Russian	revolution	Cuban	cigar		
French	restaurant				

*Methinks that Spain may have a little trouble with its image—"Spanish fly" was our celebrities' only duplication.

The Agony
and the Ecstasy

Tony Orlando

David Brenner

On the tennis court one morning at the MGM Grand Hotel in Las Vegas, I looked over the net and asked Ben Vereen to tell me THE BEST THING AND THE WORST THING HE COULD THINK OF. His answers were so good that I decided to ask some of our other celebrities the same question, always trying to catch them off guard so that their responses would be spontaneous. The people questioned were George Schlatter, David Brenner, Mort Sahl, Tony Orlando, Marilyn Chambers, and of course Ben Vereen. See if you can match the people with their impromptu replies. Ten points for each match and a 10-point bonus if you get all of them.

1. The best thing is having your health and the worst thing is having a guilty conscience.

   _____

2. War and peace! _____

3. When it's real good and when it's real bad!

   _____

4. Jacqueline Bisset and Jacqueline Bisset's husband!

   _____

5. Too much time and not enough time.

   _____

6. Some of my shows would fit in either category, but it would be too egocentric to list the first and stupid to list the second. _____

1. Ben Vereen. 2. Mort Sahl 3. Marilyn Chambers 4. David Brenner 5. Tony Orlando. 6. George Schlatter.

142

If It's Tuesday . . .

I'm lying here on my own private little beach on Mykonos, watching my sailing sloop bobbing just off shore—and the phone is ringing.

I'm lying here in Spain on a Spanish beach under the Spanish sun, with Farrah Fawcett oiled and spectacularly naked on my left and Barbara Walters oiled and fully clothed on my right—and the phone is ringing.

I wake up in New York and answer it.

This particular game is dedicated to those of you who travel for a living—those of you who have at times been forced, after staring out the hotel window for five minutes without success, to phone downstairs and ask the desk clerk where you are.

I asked Peter Ustinov whether he could name *a city outside the United States for every letter of the alphabet.* He did. In fact, running through a variety of accents, Peter came up with an incredible 119 answers in just under three minutes and 22 seconds. When he finally paused to draw breath, Peter observed that though one might have some difficulty finding a city beginning with the letter X, there are in fact over 600 listed in the index of almost any decent atlas. I decided to check up in my atlas, and you know, Mr. Ustinov was right—624 to be exact. Don't ask me how he knew that.

Peter Ustinov

For 1 point per answer, name a foreign city—or two or three—for every letter of the alphabet. Take a week or two if necessary . . .

A   Athens, Amsterdam, Algiers, Acapulco, Ankara, Anzio
B   Berlin, Buenos Aires, Bucharest, Brussels, Budapest, Bangkok
C   Caracas, Cannes, Calcutta, Casablanca, Cairo, Copenhagen
D   Dar es Salaam, Djkarta, Dublin, Dubrovnik, Dusseldorf
E   Ensenada, Edinburgh, Eliat
F   Frankfurt, Florence, Fatima, Fontainebleau
G   Grenoble, Gaza, Guatemala City, Guadalajara, Glasgow, Geneva
H   Hong Kong, Havana, Helsinki, Hamburg
I   Innsbruck, Istanbul, Inverness
J   Johannesburg, Juan Les Pins
K   Karachi, Kampur, Kuala Lumpur, Kiel, Kent
L   London, Lima, La Paz, Lisbon, Linz, Lausanne
M   Mozambique, Manila, Moscow, Mexico City, Munich, Madrid
N   Nice, Nairobi, Nancy, Nuremberg
O   Osaka, Oslo, Odessa, Oxford
P   Paris, Prague, Pisa, Phnom Penh, Peking, Palermo, Padua
Q   Quebec
R   Rome, Rangoon, Rio de Janeiro, Rotterdam
S   Sophia, Seoul, Shanghai, Singapore, Saigon, Santiago, Sydney
T   Taiwan, Tunis, Tel Aviv, Tangiers, Tokyo, Toledo, Trieste
U   Utrecht, Ulm, Uppsala
V   Venice, Vienna, Vaduz, Verona, Vosges, Villefranche Sur Mer

W Warsaw, Wurttemburg, Worms, Wien
X Xaokaoshantun, Xenia, Xinzhuangzi, Xinyi,
   Xinyu, Xinzao
Y Yokahama, Yarmouth, York, Yverdon
Z Zanzibar, Zurich, Zagreb, Zandvoort Aan Zee,
   Zeist, Zug

Here's Lookin' at You!

For this one I asked Marilu Henner and Tony Danza of "Taxi" (who have driven their share of television drunks home), Ed Asner (who, as Lou Grant, has been known to stop off to hoist a few after a hard day at the *Trib*), and New York's own Jimmy Breslin (the only man I know with a stool permanently reserved at Hurley's), to describe the state of being intoxicated— you know, all those wonderful expressions you may not find in a dictionary, like bombed, pie-eyed, smashed . . .

You can let yourself go a little bit on this one, get comfortable, pour yourself a glass of rotgut, and score 3 points for each expression you think of for the state of inebriation. If you can think of more than the celebrities' 32, give yourself an extra 10 points. Chase that with a 3-point bonus for each one you get that's in the famous folk's vocabulary.

Here's what the celebrities say for "drunk" . . .

JIMMY BRESLIN	Boring!
MARILU HENNER	Drunk
TONY DANZA	Pie-eyed
ED ASNER	Smashed

146

Tony Danza

Marilu Henner

BETTY WHITE	Three sheets to the wind
MARILU HENNER	In his cups
TONY DANZA	Zonked
ED ASNER	Out of his gourd
JIMMY BRESLIN	Polluted
MARILU HENNER	Gone to Borneo
TONY DANZA	Stoned
ED ASNER	Pissed
JIMMY BRESLIN	With a snoot full
MARILU HENNER	Swacked
ELIZABETH ASHLEY	Bombed
ED ASNER	Juiced
JAMES KOMACK	Tanked
MARILU HENNER	Inebriated
TONY DANZA	Feelin' no pain
ED ASNER	Schicker
JIMMY BRESLIN	Plastered
MARILU HENNER	Under the weather
TONY DANZA	Under the influence
ED ASNER	High
JAMES KOMACK	Sauced; jarred
MARILU HENNER	With a buzz on
TONY DANZA	Schnockered
ED ASNER	Ripped; shattered
ELIZABETH ASHLEY	With a bag on
MARILU HENNER	Soaked
BETTY WHITE	Sloshed; awash on a heavy sea; stewed to the gills!
ED ASNER	Shit-faced

Coming in Pieces

This straightforward sounding category provides an excellent example of what happens when you pose simple questions to complicated people—celebrities who have perfected the art of thinking on their feet. There are so many well-mannered answers possible in this category—pizza, pieces of eight, pie, cake, model airplanes, piecework, jigsaw puzzles—now, take a look at what my friends did to me.

Score 10 points for whatever you think of in this category. It will fit.

READ ON, MACDUFF . . .

Bill Daily

BILL DAILY	The Andrews Sisters
DAVID BRENNER	Pieces and Herb
FRED GRANDY	The Leaning Tower of Pieces
MARILU HENNER	Hollywood marriages
JED ALLEN	My life
BRETT SOMERS	Piece of tail
JIMMY BRESLIN	Xavier Hollander
JAMES KOMACK	Anybody who calls Jim Brown an asshole!
MORT SAHL	Richard Nixon's career

Shrink Tank

Here is another of those categories which Mike Douglas and Lucie Arnaz went after, right off the top of their famous heads.

I asked Mike and Lucie to name some THINGS THAT SHRINK. They gave me 16; give it your best shot and see how many you can come up with.

THINGS THAT SHRINK

1. Levi's
2. Sweaters
3. Candles
4. Soap
5. Subtraction problems
6. Division problems
7. Male appendages
8. Pygmy heads
9. Psychiatrists
10. Violets
11. The U.S. dollar
12. Hides
13. Captain Marvel
14. The Hulk
15. The Incredible Shrinking Man
16. Lily Tomlin

Fear of Flying

American Airlines
Flight #243
LA to NY

Flying, for me, is much like waking up suddenly in Milwaukee, finding your sister's name and number scrawled across the wall at the bus station, and trapped in an elevator with Alexander Haig. Flying is not my favorite thing. Since one of the few benefits of having "author" printed in your unemployment book these days is being able to deduct travel expenses, we're flying first class. Michael has been eating for five hours. If American Airlines wants to know what happened to their fourth-quarter earnings, they can find them in Michael's intestinal tract.

This flight happens to be the flight captain's last run after 38 years of flying for American. There is a carnival atmosphere on board. The CPA from Des Moines has fallen asleep after his fourth Scotch; up on the movie screen Chevy Chase is doing something very strange to Goldie Hawn. Having refused the earphones on moral principle, I can't hear what he's saying, which is the best way to watch Chevy Chase.

On a whim I ask the flight director, Bob Page, whether it might be possible to ask the first class cabin crew some question about their first-class passengers, and he arranges for everyone to gather in the lounge upstairs. The interview goes so well that I subsequently interview flight crews on Air France, P.S.A., and Pan Am planes, obtaining answers from about 25 flight attendants in all. Two of the questions I asked are which celebrities make the best passengers, and whom do you most hate to see coming through the door onto your flight? Some of the answers will surprise you.

Here are the 20 "winners" in the contest for the 10 best and 10 worst celebrity passengers. See if you can figure out who's who, in the correct order of the number of votes the candidate received, pro or con. Give yourself 4 points for each name you placed on the proper list, and a 1-point bonus if you placed the name in the correct position.

Dustin Hoffman	Mike Douglas
Steve Martin	Cindy Williams
Barbara Walters	Truman Capote
Jerry Lewis	Burt Reynolds
Helen Gurley Brown	Henry Kissinger
Barry Manilow	Lucille Ball
Diana Ross	Barbra Streisand
Johnny Carson	Merv Griffin
Roy Scheider	Joseph Wambaugh
Cher	Farrah Fawcett

THE BEST

1. _____
2. _____
3. _____
4. _____
5. _____
6. _____
7. _____
8. _____
9. _____
10. _____

THE WORST

1. _____
2. _____
3. _____
4. _____
5. _____
6. _____
7. _____
8. _____
9. _____
10. _____

Here are the responses of our 25 flight attendants:

THE BEST	THE WORST
1. Roy Scheider	1. Henry Kissinger
2. Diana Ross	2. Jerry Lewis
3. Farrah Fawcett	3. Joseph Wambaugh
4. Barbara Walters	4. Barry Manilow
5. Helen Gurley Brown	5. Lucille Ball
6. Burt Reynolds	6. Steve Martin
7. Johnny Carson	7. Cher
8. Mike Douglas	8. Dustin Hoffman
9. Merv Griffin	9. Cindy Williams
10. Truman Capote	10. Barbra Streisand

Eight women made our lists, four on each, but it's interesting to note that on the "best" list, four of the top five positions are held by women. Roy Scheider took the top honors with all four flight crews commenting that he was always pleasant, sat in his assigned seat, and never asked for nor expected any special treatment. A great deal was made of the fact that Diana Ross initiated conversation with the other passengers rather than hiding away inside of that invisible VIP bubble with which so many celebrities often surround themselves. A gorgeous, dark-eyed flight attendant for American described Dustin Hoffman as a "horny little creep," and the consensus of opinion seemed to be that Steve Martin could be a "genuine pain in the ass." Jerry Lewis and Lucille Ball were described as egomaniacs, and "generally obnoxious." Barry Manilow's name brought instant frowns.

By far the harshest comments however, were reserved for none other than Henry Kissinger, mentioned by three of the four crews as their least cooperative passenger. He was criticized for "making outrageous demands," and for "giving orders like he owned you!" I suppose that once you've had your own Air Force jumbo jet, even first class seems like steerage.

Some others who were not held in great esteem, but who didn't receive enough complaints to make our "bottom ten" were Marlo Thomas, ("she took some poor guy's seat when he got up to go to the john and then wouldn't give it up") and Jeff Conaway of "Taxi." One of the senior flight directors told us that when he approached Conaway to make his "Welcome aboard, may we book a limousine for you in New York, sir?" speech (a courtesy extended not only to celebrities but to everyone in first class), Conaway interrupted him with "Do I have to be bored by this crap?" Among those receiving single but vehement votes for the turkey list were Goldie Hawn, Flip Wilson, Rod Stewart, Senator S. I. Hayakawa and Gloria Steinem.

As for occupations, the "best" list contains three acting types, with two thespians in the "worst" category. There is one author on each list, along with one singer on the positive side and three on the negative. The "best" list also harbors one editor/publisher, one television newsperson, and three talk show hosts. The "worst" is completed by that ex-secretary of state and three comics.

Personally, I was fascinated that not only did Carson, Douglas, and Griffin all make the "best" list, but that they ended up within two places of each other. It may have something to do with all that practice at dealing with strangers. It's also intriguing that the "worst" list is dominated by Mr. Martin, Mr. Lewis, and Ms. Ball, people who are famous for making us laugh and feel good.

Once these results were in hand, I decided to

show the list of names to a number of other celebrities we were interviewing. They were asked to try to place the celebrity passengers in the correct list, just as you have done.

Among the ten celebrities that we queried, not one failed to choose Burt Reynolds, Farrah Fawcett, or Roy Scheider as likely candidates for the "best" list. Even more revealing may be the fact that every single one of those same celebrities identified Cher, Henry Kissinger, Jerry Lewis, Lucille Ball, and Barbra Streisand as sure bets for the "hate to see come through the door" department. None of our celebrities guessed that Dustin Hoffman or Barry Manilow would be on the "worst" list, and only two thought that Cindy Williams would end up there. The majority were surprised, however, that Capote and Barbara Walters did so well.

The average steward or stewardess deals every day with people like you and me who have already had it with smiling redcaps, incompetent car rental companies, and constipated customs officials.

Flight attendants are blamed for rising airline costs, shrinking seat widths, and the common occurrence that there is only enough "Chicken à la Fernando Lamas" for the first three rows.

With that in mind, I would like to thank the flight crews of Air France, PSA, and Pan American, who were kind enough to assist us with this informal survey. A special thanks goes to the New York-based crew of American Airlines, flight 243, who gathered in the topside lounge that day and gave us some of our most memorable quotes. Flight director was Bob Page, and the flight attendants were Kevin McGuiness, Judy Tull, Mike Mendoza, Robin Gallo, and Suzanne Russell.

That Certain Someone

For each of us, I am sure, there is hidden among our childhood memories some person whom we would like to go back and see again. First loves, when we were five going on six, the kid who made life miserable when we were six and hoping to be seven . . . I wonder how they'd look now, and what we'd say to them.

This is exactly what I asked 15 celebrities: If you could do it, whom would you like to go back and see again, and why? Some of them had to think about the answer for a while, whereas others knew immediately whom they would want to see again if they could turn back the hands of time. See if you can figure out which celebrities go with which memories. The celebrities are:

Art Buchwald	George Carlin
Ray Charles	Ben Vereen
Dr. Joyce Brothers	Jimmy Breslin
Patrick Terrail	Laurie Walters
Mort Sahl	David Brenner
Francesco Scavullo	Tony Orlando
Ed Asner	Gay Talese
Elizabeth Ashley	

You deserve 10 points for each match you get; if you get all of them you definitely have special powers! Answers at the bottom of the page 157.

1. _____ Sam Stefano at P.S. 35 in Hollis, New York. He always used to beat the hell out of me after school. Now that I have some money I can afford to hire someone to beat the hell out of him!

2. _____ Bobby Darin, just for a minute!

3. _____ My mother, You know, she never got to see any of the good things that happened to me, and I'd just like her to know that I did OK.

4. _____ Mr. Johnson; he was my gym teacher in the fifth grade. I'd like to go back and look him in the eye and tell him that gym has absolutely nothing to do with life.

5. _____ There was this little Eurasian girl who sat in front of me in the second grade. I was always afraid to talk to her. Her name was Barbara. I still wonder how I could have been so captivated by her beauty in the second grade.

6. _____ There was such a person, a golden girl from grade school whom, thirty years later, I did look up. I don't recommend this to other people. I'm sure that if the roles were reversed, we would prove equally disappointing.

7. _____ Myself, because I was my favorite!

8. _____ I don't even remember his name, I've done such a good job of pushing him out of my mind—but his nickname was Poopsy. We were studying at Dartmouth together, and he was the only man I ever wanted that I couldn't get. He wanted someone who was rich or came from a family that could help him. I'd love to go back

now and find that s.o.b. and tell him, thanks but no thanks!

9. _____ It might be interesting to go back and find your first love, the love that will never die . . . marry her, and kill it once and for all!

10. _____ Oh boy, yeah, the kids from the neighborhood—Sabu, Diablo, Killer. I'd like to see Sabu again. He owes me two dollars and fifty cents. He took it from me one day on the way to school. He and fifteen other guys. On second thought, maybe I don't want to see Sabu again.

11. _____ I'd like to go back and find Heidi and punch her out.

12. _____ Billy Canon. He could run faster than anyone and I could never catch him. He owes me one.

13. _____ Sally Quinn. We were schoolmates and she was the great love of my young life. She wouldn't have anything to do with me because I was so short then. I'm taller now than she is, but she's married to Ben Bradlee of the *Washington Post,* and I doubt that Ben would be willing to give her up!

14. _____ Just the people up there on the silver screen!

15. _____ Nobody! I see everybody every day. I never left where I grew up.

1. Art Buchwald 2. Tony Orlando 3. Ray Charles 4. David Brenner 5. Ed Asner 6. Gay Talese 7. George Carlin 8. Dr. Joyce Brothers 9. Mort Sahl 10. Ben Vereen 11. Laurie Walters 12. Elizabeth Ashley 13. Patrick Terrail 14. Francesco Scavullo 15. Jimmy Breslin

If I Knew What He Knew ✳

The Russian Tea Room
Fifty-seventh Street
New York

Take the unlikely premise that it is somehow possible to look a person in the eye and suddenly to know everything that person knows—the total thought process behind every accomplishment and failure. On the basis of this premise I asked Ben Vereen, David Brenner, Ed Asner, Dick Van Patten, Jed Allen, Peter Ustinov, and Mort Sahl whose mind they might like totally to comprehend or to borrow for a day.

See if you can put yourself into their minds as you try to decipher the surprising list of famous people whose mental set the celebrities find fascinating. Score 10 points for each correct match and give yourself a 30-point bonus if you are clairvoyant and get them all. Hint: Two celebrities named two famous personages whose mind they'd like to penetrate.

Ben Vereen

David Brenner

Ed Asner

Peter Ustinov

Mort Sahl

CELEBRITIES	MINDS
Ben Vereen	Mr. Steeple
David Brenner	Einstein
Ed Asner	Lee Harvey Oswald
Dick Van Patten	Bill "Bojangles" Robinson
	Joe Louis
Jed Allen	God
Peter Ustinov	Orson Welles
Mort Sahl	Clarence Darrow
	Lee Harvey Oswald

ED ASNER   **Lee Harvey Oswald,** because I would like to find out what really happened that morning in Dallas.

JED ALLEN   **Orson Welles!** Without a doubt. The rest of us could be considered geniuses if we had some of the ideas he must have thought of and rejected for being "not good enough"!

DICK VAN PATTEN   **Joe Louis.** Just to understand the instincts that enable a man to triumph over the likes of a Max Schmelling or a Jim Braddock.

PETER USTINOV   **Ovid.** Roman poet, 43 BC to AD 17, *Publius Ovidius Naso.* It might be nice to just sit around and chat.

BEN VEREEN   **Einstein** and **Bill "Bojangles" Robinson!**

MORT SAHL   **Clarence Darrow!** Can you imagine knowing whether he was really that sure of his own abilities?

DAVID BRENNER   **God** or **Mr. Steeple.** Mr. Steeple ran the candy store on the corner where I grew up. God's mind might be even more interesting, but Mr. Steeple sure knew a lot of great stuff.

AWKWARD
MOMENTS

Whoops!
(When, Where, and Under What Circumstances Did You Lose Your Virginity?)

I must confess that it seems a little strange in this era of sexual liberation to hear people talking about "losing their virginity," as if they had inadvertently misplaced it. I never met a woman, or man for that matter, who didn't remember exactly what they had done with it!

That is precisely the question I posed—how did you lose it?—to Marilyn Chambers, Lucie Arnaz, George Hamilton, Marilu Henner, Elizabeth Ashley, Peter Ustinov, Jed Allen, and David Brenner.

For most of us, that special moment of first love is forever engraved in memory . . . or fantasy. Think back to those thrilling days of yesteryear, to that one time when you came home with less than what you went out with. Then think of our celebrities, and try to match each to his or her own loss of innocence.

Take 10 points for each match and a 10-point bonus if you get them all.

George Hamilton   Marilyn Chambers
Elizabeth Ashley   Jed Allen
Lucie Arnaz   Marilu Henner
Peter Ustinov   David Brenner

1. I didn't lose it, darlin', I threw it away!_____

2. With a 54-year-old part-time pro in Parkersburg, West Virginia. I contributed to her retirement fund! _____

3. At his place, in a very chic apartment, on the sofa. But right in the middle of everything I kicked over his favorite lamp, and that was the end of that. _____

4. In the backseat of your car! Actually, I was 16 and it was with a football player. It happened accidentally when we fell off the couch!

   _____

5. It was the night of the moon walk, in July—July 20, 1969, and I lost my virginity standing up in the shower, because you know good Catholic schoolgirls are into everything but penetration, because that's the mortal sin and everything else is venial. So I was already into taking showers but not into anything else, and it just got too slippery to resist! That's how I lost my virginity—one small step for, you know . . . _____

6. Tomorrow at four o'clock—that is, if she shows up! _____

7. In St. Petersburg, Florida. I was 12 and she was 36. She ran an art gallery—she wasn't a hooker. Just a couple of years ago I discovered that a kid I grew up with lost his at the same age, to the same nice lady in the back room of that same gallery! We called him Buddy then. You know him as Burt Reynolds." _____

8. Embarrassingly late in life. _____

Here are what our eight celebrities told us:

ELIZABETH ASHLEY "I didn't lose it darlin' . . . I threw it away!"

JED ALLEN "With a fifty-four-year-old part-time pro in Parkersburg, West Virginia. I contributed to her retirement fund!"

LUCIE ARNAZ "At his place, in a very chic apartment, on the sofa, but right in the middle of everything I kicked over his favorite lamp and that was the end of that!"

MARILYN CHAMBERS "In the back seat of your car! Actually, I was sixteen and it was with a football player. It happened accidentally when we fell off the couch!"

MARILU HENNER "It was the night of the moon-walk, in July—O.K., July 20th, 1969 and I lost my virginity standing up in the shower, because you know good Catholic school girls are into everything but penetration because that's the mortal sin, everything else is venial, so I was already into taking showers but not into anything else and it just got too slippery to resist! That's how I lost my virginity, one small step for, you know!

DAVID BRENNER "Tomorrow! At four o'clock! That is . . . if she shows up!"

GEORGE HAMILTON "St. Petersburg, Florida. I was twelve and she was thirty-six. She ran an art gallery. She wasn't a hooker, but just a couple of years ago I discovered that a kid I grew up with lost his, at the same age, to the same nice lady in the back room of that same gallery! We called him 'Buddy' then, you know him as Burt Reynolds!"

PETER USTINOV "Embarrassingly late in life!"

Oh Yeah?

Danny's
Fifth Avenue and
Fifty-eighth Street
New York

This time we asked our celebrities to reach back into their misspent youths to come up with curses that contain no curse words—expletives that you don't have to delete. Have you ever heard of the native tribes whose pitched battle with their enemies consist of hurling insults and curses at each other? I wouldn't want to go up against our celebrity team—but perhaps you can outcurse them.

Score 3 points for each curse and a 10-point bonus if you come up with more than 30 inventive curses.

GEORGE CARLIN   Go take an aeronautical intercourse through an animated pastry!

DR. JOYCE BROTHERS   May you grow like an onion—with your head in the ground!

ELIZABETH ASHLEY   Up yours! You nurd, you frump, you dork—and of course, the ever popular "Eat it!" You running dog lackey of American imperialism!

BETTY WHITE   Sufferin' succotash! The same to you fella!

PETER MARSHALL   Go take a flyin' leap at a rollin' donut!

Ben Vereen

MARILU HENNER   Sit on it! Kiss this!

TONY DANZA   Shove it!

FRED GRANDY   Your mother wears combat boots!

DAVID BRENNER   In your ear! Honk this! Go suck an egg!

GENE RAYBURN   Drop dead!

JIMMY BRESLIN   Blow it out the other end!

DICK MARTIN   So's your old man!

BILL CULLEN   Your father's moustache!

JAMES KOMACK   You want to buy some pictures of your sister?

BEN VEREEN   Go take a long walk on a short pier!

BILL DAILY   In your hat!

TONY ORLANDO   Go fly a kite!

Gesundheit!

CBS Studio City
Hollywood

Ed Asner is the person who made me realize that this project could be contagious. I had contacted his executive assistant, Alex Street, with the request to interview Ed and had enclosed a few examples of the kind of question I might ask him.

Very soon the phone rang in my office and it was Ed Asner. He wanted to know when I wanted to do the interview.

Anytime he was ready, I told him.

He said he was ready.

Twenty minutes later we were sitting in his dressing room at CBS knee-deep in answers. Forty-five minutes later, when I pulled out the release for him to sign, Mr. Asner shook his head, motioning for his secretary, Becky Chandler, to lock the door. "I'm not going to sign that yet," he grinned, "give me another question!"

The next day, Arthur Price, vice president of MTM (Mary Tyler Moore's production company) and the man who had graciously arranged for my original contact with Mr. Asner, called and said, "What the hell have you done to Ed? He stopped me in the hall this morning and wanted to know whether I could name fifty things you have to get undressed to do!"

Ed Asner

I asked Ed to name human sounds, and he came up with more than 50, which is going to be difficult to top. But try anyway.

Be very quiet for a moment. Listen . . . to others . . . to yourself . . . go! Score 3 points for each human sound you think of. Then compare with Ed's list.

To a veritable concert of accompanying sound effects, Ed Asner gave us the following responses:

Snoring
Sneezes
Snorts and sniffles
Whistling
The rumble of one's stomach
Belch and burp
Blowing your nose
Humming
Cracking your knuckles
Snapping your fingers
Strange footsteps in the night
Cough
Fart
Screams
Crying
Laughter
The thrill of applause
The horror of boos
Gargling

The sound of bad dentures
Spitting
Being slapped
Wheezing
Old people's bones cracking
Moaning when you're in pain
Moaning when you're in something else!
Hiccups
Kissing
Sighs
Inhale
Exhale
Fornicating
Ohhh!
Aghhhh!
Whewwwww!
Mmmmmmm!

Eek!
Smacking your lips
Groaning
Gasping
Giggling
Swallowing
Tapping your foot
Chewing
The old raspberry
Scratching
Teeth chattering
Clicking your tongue
Hissing
Breathing heavy
Gnashing your teeth
Popping your jaw
Cutting your nails
Being squeaky clean
The sound of your heartbeat

Help!   ✳

Only a total fool would claim to be afraid of nothing. Muhammad Ali knows fear! John Wayne was afraid in *The Sands of Iwo Jima*. I am afraid of being found dead, or worse, of Charlie Bronson coming home unexpectedly . . . afraid of chicken tettrazini, angry Corsican sailors, and independent women who drive Datsun Z's—though not necessarily in that order.

One night when the moon was high over Italy, author Gay Talese just happened to mention something he was afraid of. That led to an interesting conversation, and it was just a matter of time before I started asking everyone I met about their special fears. Strangely, this question was a favorite with our brave celebrities, though some of the frightening things they named seemed distinctly less frightful than others. Here you have a chance to find out the private phobias of some of the world's brightest celebrities. But first see if you can guess exactly who is afraid of what.

Score 10 points for each correct match, and take a 10-point bonus if you get more than half right. The answers are at the bottom of the next page.

David Brenner

170

a. George Carlin
b. Judith Krantz
c. Jimmy Breslin
d. Charles Aznavour
e. Elizabeth Ashley
f. Dr. Joyce Brothers
g. Gay Talese
h. Madeline Kahn
i. Art Buchwald
j. Marilyn Chambers

k. Ben Vereen
l. Ed Asner
m. David Brenner
n. Peter Ustinov
o. Muhammad Ali
p. Orson Welles
q. Marilu Henner
r. Tony Orlando
s. Steve Allen
t. Francesco Scavullo

HERE ARE THE FEARS . . .

1. _____ Other people's dogs.
2. _____ Unemployment.
3. _____ Being predictable.
4. _____ Being left out of the *New York Times* obituary column because of tight space that day.
5. _____ Authoritarian figures.
6. _____ Flying.
7. _____ Bee-stings and defective vibrators.
8. _____ Being poor. Being poor again wouldn't bother me too much, but always being poor, never knowing what it is like to be anything but poor, that would scare the hell out of me!
9. _____ War and canned tuna.
10. _____ Bette Midler.
11. _____ Indira Gandhi.
12. _____ Everything.
13. _____ Rats! Wild ones, though I'm not all that choked up about cute little white laboratory ones either!
14. _____ A psychologist once announced, "The only

two really instinctive fears in humans are of loud noises and of falling. What are you afraid of?" I answered, "I have a great fear of making a loud noise while falling!"

15. _____ Me.

16. _____ Being dependent on somebody . . . anybody!

17. _____ Not being in love.

18. _____ Airborne syphilis germs.

19. _____ Driving alone on unknown places where I haven't parked before. I absolutely refuse to do it after dark. I have never driven on a freeway.

20. _____ It would take your whole book to list them! I always look at the dark side, it's all bad. I never look up because I know that the second I do, it's going to rain. Most of all, though, I'm afraid of missing something. That terrifies me!

1. n. 2. k. 3. g. 4. i. 5. b.
6. o. 7. j. 8. m. 9. l.
10. r. 11. p. 12. t. 13. f.
14. s. 15. q. 16. e. 17. d.
18. a. 19. b. 20. c.

172

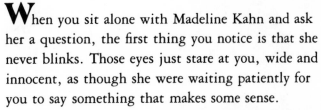

Yuk!

When you sit alone with Madeline Kahn and ask her a question, the first thing you notice is that she never blinks. Those eyes just stare at you, wide and innocent, as though she were waiting patiently for you to say something that makes some sense.

You ask Madeline to name something she wouldn't want to find in her sleeping bag, and she doesn't answer. You ask her to describe Gene Wilder's technique as a romantic leading man, and she doesn't answer. You ask her to tell you something that she wouldn't want to touch, and she blinks once and says: "An oyster!" A perfect answer to all three questions.

Thirty-two replies to this question were deemed worthy of inclusion in the roster. You get 3 points for just about anything you think of, and a 3-point bonus if you happen to think of something listed here.

Here are the celebrities' responses. Touching, aren't they . . .

Peter Marshall

173

Marilu Henner

Tony Danza

Elizabeth Ashley

MADELINE KAHN	An oyster.
ART BUCHWALD	A 10-foot pole, the center rail on the "E" train in Queens, and any wine before its time.
LUCIE ARNAZ	Slimy stuff!
BEN VEREEN	The sun.
FRANCESCO SCAVULLO	Almost everything.
TONY ORLANDO	A rabid dog.
NADIA COMANECI	Snakes and spiders.
BOBBY SHORT	Leftovers.
REGINE	This question.
PETER USTINOV	A moving bus.
ELIZABETH ASHLEY	Richard Nixon.
ED ASNER	Snails or slugs or old streetwalkers.
BOBBY VINTON	Phyllis Diller.
LAURIE WALTERS	Dog doo-doo.
BETTY WHITE	Any part of Yasir Arafat.
JED ALLEN	An untouchable.
ROBERT SHIELDS	Wet paint.
ROLF HARRIS	Tapioca pudding.
MARILU HENNER	There must be something . . .
TONY DANZA	People with contagious diseases.
FRED GRANDY	The Lennon Sisters.
GEORGE CARLIN	Eel Jello.
PETER MARSHALL	Karl Malden.
DR. JOYCE BROTHERS	Cockroaches.
MARK GOODSON	Electric wires, scorpions, heroin.

Ben Vereen

GENE RAYBURN
DAVID BRENNER
An elephant's testicles.
Doc Severinson, a live
barracuda's tooth,
Sonny Scungilli, Bella
Abzug, Tricia Nixon,
boiling water, a
Shriner and New
Jersey!